THE
REAL ESTATE
INVESTOR'S

Tax Strategy Guide

- MAXIMIZE TAX BENEFITS AND WRITE-OFFS
- IMPLEMENT MONEY-SAVING STRATEGIES
- AVOID COSTLY MISTAKES
- PROTECT YOUR INVESTMENT
- BUILD YOUR WEALTH

TYLER D. KRAEMER

and TAMMY H. KRAEMER

BUSINESS
Avon, Massachusetts

Copyright © 2009 by Tyler D. Kraemer and Tammy H. Kraemer
This book, or parts thereof, may not be reproduced in any
form without permission from the publisher; exceptions
are made for brief excerpts used in published reviews.

Published by Adams Business, an imprint of Adams Media, an F+W Media Company
57 Littlefield Street, Avon, MA 02322
www.adamsmedia.com

ISBN 10: 1-59869-760-9
ISBN 13: 978-1-59869-760-5

Printed in Canada.

J   I   H   G   F   E   D   C   B   A

Library of Congress Cataloging-in-Publication Data
available from the publisher.

This publication is designed to provide accurate and authoritative information with regard to
the subject matter covered. It is sold with the understanding that the publisher is not engaged
in rendering legal, accounting, or other professional advice. If legal advice or other expert
assistance is required, the services of a competent professional person should be sought.
    —From a *Declaration of Principles* jointly adopted by a Committee of the
    American Bar Association and a Committee of Publishers and Associations

Many of the designations used by manufacturers and sellers to distinguish their product are
claimed as trademarks. Where those designations appear in this book and Adams Media was
aware of a trademark claim, the designations have been printed with initial capital letters.

RealTick® graphics used with permission of Townsend Analytics, Ltd. © 1986–2008
Townsend Analytics, Ltd. All rights reserved. RealTick is a registered trademark of
Townsend Analytics, Ltd. Any unauthorized reproduction, alteration, or use of RealTick
is strictly prohibited. Authorized use of RealTick does not constitute an endorsement by
Townsend Analytics of this book. Townsend Analytics does not guarantee the accuracy
or warrant any representations made in this book.

This book is available at quantity discounts for bulk purchases.
For information, please call 1-800-289-0963.

Contents

DISCLAIMER: The intent of this book is to provide competent, useful information about the subject matter covered. However, this book is purchased with the understanding that neither the authors nor the publisher are engaged in rendering specific accounting, financial, insurance, investment, legal, tax, or other professional advice and services. If the reader requires such advice and/or services, a competent professional should be consulted. It should also be noted that the strategies described in this book may not be suitable for every individual, are not guaranteed or warranted to produce any particular results, and that relevant laws vary from state to state. No warranty is made with respect to the accuracy or completeness of the information contained herein. The authors and the publisher specifically disclaim any responsibility for any liability, loss, or risk, personal or otherwise, which is incurred as a consequence, directly or indirectly, of the use and application of any of the contents of this book.

IRS CIRCULAR 230 DISCLOSURE: TO ENSURE COMPLIANCE WITH REQUIREMENTS IMPOSED BY THE INTERNAL REVENUE SERVICE, WE INFORM YOU THAT ANY U.S. FEDERAL TAX ADVICE CONTAINED IN THIS BOOK IS NOT INTENDED OR WRITTEN TO BE USED, AND CANNOT BE USED, FOR THE PURPOSE OF AVOIDING PENALTIES UNDER THE INTERNAL REVENUE CODE OR PROMOTING, MARKETING, OR RECOMMENDING TO ANOTHER PARTY ANY TRANSACTION OR MATTER ADDRESSED HEREIN.

Dedication and Acknowledgments

Thank you to Ed Claflin and Adams Media for believing that two heads are better than one even when those two heads are married. We would each like to thank our coauthor for limitless energy and encouragement through another project together. May we continue to look outward together in the same direction and keep our sense of humor.

A very special thank-you to the following professionals:

Robert A. Crandall, **CPA**, for contributing his finely tuned tax and accounting expertise, giving his time during tax season, and reviewing the chapters for everything from correcting our accounting vocabulary to making sure we included the most recent tax rules and decisions.

Michael W. Deen, **Esq.**, contributing author, for sharing his knowledge of good planning through years of helping clients achieve their personal, estate, and business planning goals. Michael provided the original draft of Chapter 11 on estate planning and charitable giving strategies for real estate.

John S. Benson, **Esq.**, for being a thoughtful mentor and sharing strategies and stories from his extensive experience advising clients on real estate, business, and estate planning matters.

Thank you also to our two amazing sons, Kai and Cary, for teaching us why people get so attached to their homes; Gregory Daries for transforming complex ideas into simple graphics; Nancy Smelser for considerable administrative assistance; Rachel Reynolds for keeping our two energetic boys busy while we write; Judy Fogler for teaching that laughter improves all projects; and Sandy and Dorothy Kraemer for providing never-ending inspiration and love to our family.

Preface

*It won't be the economy that will do in investors; it will
be the investors themselves.*

—*Warren Buffett*

As we write this book the United States economy seems headed
toward a recession. Some say it is already here and others think
we can fend it off. On the real estate front, it is clear that the housing
market is in a slump. Commercial real estate is fairing a little better, but
office vacancies are starting to rise. Inquiries about how to avoid foreclosure are more common than those about how to structure new deals.

So why are we writing a book about tax strategies for real estate
investors? The tax strategies that are the focus of this book are not tied
to economic conditions. When conditions are good they can significantly
enhance investment return, and when economic conditions are bad they
may be the only source of investment return. Real estate market cycles
remind us that real estate is a long-term investment. There are always
good deals out there for the patient and informed investor. In fact, some
argue that the best deals come when the market is down.

Regardless of economic conditions, the Internal Revenue Code can,
ironically, be the key to building wealth with real estate. It contains many
provisions that reward real estate ownership by reducing, deferring, and
sometimes even eliminating taxes for those who invest in and own real
estate. Investors who do their homework and use these tax code strategies can weather economic conditions and continue to build wealth.

The challenge is that the IRS does not make it easy to defer or eliminate taxes. Even some of the most popular real estate tax strategies, such
as like-kind exchanges, require understanding complex rules and requirements. The first step in using tax strategies is knowing about them, and

the second is planning for them. Only then can you take the third step of working with your tax advisor to implement your strategies.

This book is not meant to provide tax advice for any particular situation but to reveal tax and legal strategies that can be used by real estate investors. Part One covers strategies for keeping more income by using expense and loss deductions, including depreciation. Part Two focuses on how to defer or eliminate taxes when selling real estate by using the principal residence exclusion, installment sales, like-kind exchanges, and tenant-in-common investment. Part Three focuses on risk reduction and explains how to protect your assets and use the right ownership structures for holding real estate. Part Four combines real estate and family matters, such as estate planning, family limited partnerships, and stepped-up basis. Finally, Part Five addresses several special topics, like investing in real estate with an IRA and owning foreign real estate.

The breadth of information covered in this book is significant, but it is required reading for any real estate investor or anyone who advises them. The difference between owning real estate and being a real estate investor is that an investor knows how to maximize the investment. A big part of maximizing an investment is proper tax planning. What good is buying low and selling high if a majority of the gain is lost to taxes? We sincerely hope that this book will introduce you to strategies that you can use to build wealth, save taxes, protect your assets, and create a more secure financial future.

CHAPTER 1

Real Estate and Taxes: The Groundwork

Great things are not done by impulse, but by a series of small things brought together.

—Vincent Van Gogh

Real estate is on everyone's mind. More people are visiting real estate-related websites than ever before. In fact, we are so tuned in to real estate that the market cycles affect our mood. When the real estate market is down we worry. When the market swings back up we feel confident. Despite all the attention, few real estate investors really know how to plan and manage their investments for maximum profit. Smart investors know that there are three primary ways to build wealth with real estate:

1. Appreciation
2. Cash flow
3. Tax advantages

This book focuses on the tax advantages. We outline tax and legal strategies used by successful real estate investors to build and keep their real estate wealth. Some of these strategies are simple and some are complex. The great thing about tax and legal strategies is that they are not tied to market conditions. You can use these strategies in conjunction with smart investing to achieve positive results in any kind of market. First, however, you need to understand the basics of real estate and taxation that lay the groundwork for success.

1

OUR TAX SYSTEM

Congress passed the first income tax around 1861 to pay for the Civil War. It was 3 percent! Since that time the tax laws and rates have seen dramatic changes. The Internal Revenue Code (the tax code) and the rules, regulations, procedures, tax court opinions, and other materials that supplement the tax code fill volumes. The most recent major changes were made as part of the Jobs and Growth Tax Relief and Reconciliation Act of 2003 (2003 Act). The 2003 Act reduced both the capital gain tax rate and the dividend tax rate to 15 percent. Both are set to expire January 1, 2011. Tax changes are inevitable, especially changes to tax rates, but many basic concepts remain the same.

Types of Income

There are three general categories of income in our federal tax system:

➤ Tax-free income
➤ Ordinary income
➤ Capital gain

Tax-Free Income

It is not hard to guess which one is the best type of income. Tax-free income includes income that is either technically not an increase in wealth or is simply labeled as tax free in the tax code because of a government policy. Examples of tax-free income can include borrowed money (typically not considered an increase in wealth) or interest on municipal and state government bonds (treated as tax-free income because of policy decisions).

Ordinary Income

The most common, though usually the least favorable, type of income is ordinary earned income. Ordinary earned income includes income from the performance of personal services, for example, wages, salaries, and other forms of compensation. Other ordinary income includes interest and certain types of dividends.

There are currently six graduated ordinary income rates for individual taxpayers ranging from 10 to 35 percent. A corporation's ordinary income is also taxed at graduated rates ranging from 15 to 35 percent. Estates and trust tax rates on ordinary income also range from 15 to 35 percent, although the rates graduate faster. These graduated rates mean ordinary income is taxed in a progressive manner: the higher your income, the higher your tax rate. A taxpayer's highest marginal income tax rate is the highest rate applied to his income. A taxpayer's effective income tax rate is the average rate that applies to all his income.

There are also other taxes charged on certain income. Most states impose a tax on the federal taxable income of individuals, corporations, estates, and trusts. Depending on the source of the ordinary income, there may be other federal taxes as well. Earned income, like salaries and wages, are subject to FICA (Social Security and Medicare) taxes, which take an additional 7.65 percent of an employee's salary and a full 15.3 percent of a self-employed person's income, subject to certain limits that seem to change annually. Investment income, including interest, dividends, and rent, is generally not subject to FICA taxes. So, at least with respect to cash-in-pocket now, rental income from real estate is typically preferred to wages.

Capital Gain

The final type of income and the most important for real estate investors is capital gain. Capital gain results from the sale or exchange of assets used in a trade or business or held for investment, such as rental property. Capital gains are either short term or long term. *Long-term capital gains* come from assets that are held for more than one year (that is, one year and a day), and *short-term capital gains* come from assets held for one year or less. The general rule is that long-term capital gain recognized by individuals is subject to a maximum rate of 15 percent and short-term gain is taxed at the ordinary income rates.

However, there are important exceptions that could change the ultimate rates applied to any gain. Two major exceptions are the recapture of depreciation at 25 percent and the alternative minimum tax. Another exception applies to corporations. Corporations do not receive the lower long-term capital gain rate; short-term and long-term capital gain recognized by corporations are essentially taxed like ordinary income. Plus, corporations can only apply capital losses against capital gains, not ordinary income.

As you can see, different types of income are taxed differently. Income from real estate investing offers several tax advantages.

1. *Leverage*. Borrowing money to purchase property is a tax-free event that allows you to build wealth through leveraging.
2. *No FICA*. Most rent from income-producing properties is not subject to FICA like wage income (exceptions include hotel or motel rentals).
3. *Low tax rate*. Gain on the sale of a property held for more than one year can qualify for the lowest capital gain tax rate.

Alternative Minimum Tax

One possible exception to many of the tax strategies covered in this book is the big bad alternative minimum tax (AMT). The AMT is an extra tax some people have to pay on top of their regular income tax. The original policy behind the AMT was to prevent high-income taxpayers from paying little or no taxes by using deductions and exclusions. Over time the AMT has expanded, and it now impacts many taxpayers who do not have high income.

The AMT provides an alternative method for calculating your income tax. If this AMT calculation produces a higher tax liability than the regular calculation, then the taxpayer must pay the higher amount. Unfortunately, the AMT catches a lot of real estate investors because a year with a large capital gain (for example, from the sale of a property) can create an AMT liability.

Whether it is the AMT, the recapture of depreciation, or something else, there will almost always be exceptions to the general rules and strategies covered in this book. For this reason, it is critical to work with a competent tax advisor and have a tax professional complete and file your tax return. Another reason why real estate investors need good tax advisors is that while income or gain from real estate activities usually receives better tax treatment than other investments, your bottom line will still be reduced by taxes unless you can find a way to defer or eliminate taxes.

When faced with potentially taxable income and gain, there are essentially three options: pay the tax bill, find a way to defer the tax, or eliminate the tax. The remaining chapters in this book focus on legitimate methods of deferring or eliminating tax, but there are a few more tax concepts that you need to know about before we can dig into actual strategies for tax deferral or elimination.

Important Tax Concepts

Choosing the right tax strategy depends on understanding your options and how those options are shaped by the way certain activities are characterized or treated for tax purposes. The tax code is full of tests that determine how activities are characterized and how gains or losses are treated. Following are important tax concepts that should give you the vocabulary necessary to make the most of the strategies in the rest of the book.

Realization Versus Recognition

The most fundamental tax concept for real estate investors to understand may be the difference between *realization* and *recognition* of gain. Gain or loss is usually realized at the time a property is sold or exchanged. Gain or loss is recognized when it is included in or deducted from gross income for tax purposes. We usually think of realization and recognition as occurring simultaneously. Earned income from wages or self-employment is typically realized and recognized in the year in which it was earned.

Real estate investing offers a unique opportunity to separate the timing of recognition from realization. As you will see, the primary goal of several strategies in this book is to delay the recognition of gain. For example, in a like-kind exchange (see Chapter 7 for details) a taxpayer may realize gain when he exchanges one property for another, but he does not recognize or pay taxes on the gain at the time of the exchange.

To see the benefits of delaying recognition, consider the following simplified example. Chris purchased an investment property five years ago for $300,000. He plans to sell it now for $500,000. Upon the sale he

OPTION AGREEMENTS

Selling someone an option to buy your property puts cash in your pocket but can avoid recognition of gain. The option agreement must be drafted properly, including a right to a refund if the option buyer does not follow through and acquire the property.

will realize a $200,000 gain. This realized gain will also be recognized, and he will owe at least $30,000 in taxes. If Chris exchanges the property in a like-kind exchange, instead of selling it, he will still realize a $200,000 gain but will not have to pay the $30,000 in taxes since recognition is delayed until a later time.

Adjusted Basis

Another important concept real estate investors need to know is *adjusted basis*. Adjusted basis is important because it is used to determine your taxable gain or loss. Taxable gain is the amount you realize from a sale or exchange of property that is more than its adjusted basis. The adjusted basis of a property is your original or cost basis plus certain additions and minus certain deductions. A buyer's cost basis can be summarized as the buyer's cost to purchase the property. The cost basis includes amounts paid in cash or other assets and certain debt incurred. It also includes broker commissions, closing and title fees, and capitalized legal and accounting fees. Adjustments to the cost basis are made over time for certain costs incurred, like capital improvements and depreciation. Figure 1.1 shows a typical example of adjusted basis as determined at the time of sale.

Investor Versus Dealer

The label you are given by the IRS can have a significant impact on your bottom line and the tax strategies available to you. Real estate investors need to know the difference between investor and dealer activities. In most cases, the best tax rates and advantages go to investors.

Unfortunately, investor versus dealer status is one of those murky areas that get tax professionals tongue tied. We think of a dealer as someone who holds property primarily for sale to customers in the ordinary course of his trade or business (for example, a subdivider or developer). An investor, on the other hand, is someone who holds property primarily for appreciation.

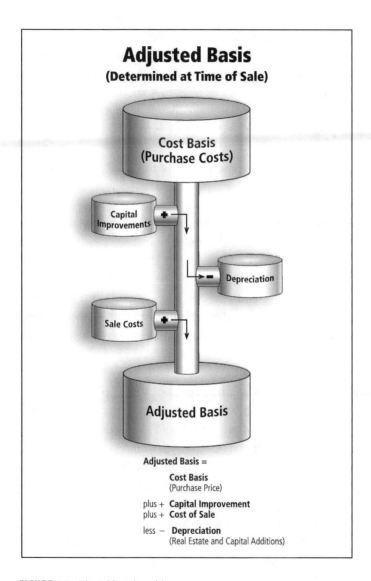

FIGURE 1.1 Adjusted Basis (sample)

There are no hard and fast rules, but following are some of the more common factors that the tax courts have used to decide whether someone is an investor or dealer:

➤ *Number of sales activities.* A person who makes multiple sales in a single tax year may appear more like a dealer.

➤ *Primary intent for which the property was acquired.* Your intent at the time you bought the property is a big issue for the IRS, even though it is very hard to know what is in someone's mind. If you intend to hold the property for appreciation, you are probably an investor. If you intend to resell the property, you are probably a dealer.

➤ *Activity of the owner in connection with the sales.* Regular and ongoing advertisements make you appear more like a dealer, as does having a business office dedicated to sales.

➤ *Nature and extent of owner's other business.* If your primary source of income is from property sales, you appear more like a dealer. If you have another business that rises to the level of being an occupational undertaking, then you look more like an investor.

➤ *Extent of improvements made to the property.* Making extensive improvements, such as subdividing, paving, or utilities, to the property may signal that the taxpayer bought the property for resale and is a dealer.

The label is important since different tax rates apply to investors and dealers. Investors get to apply the currently lower long-term capital gain rate on gain from the sale of properties held longer than one year. In contrast, dealers must normally pay ordinary income tax rates on gain, which could also trigger self-employment taxes. The 2008 maximum tax rate on ordinary income is 35 percent, more than double the maximum rate on long-term capital gain of 15 percent.

In addition, certain tax strategies are only available to investors. Only investors can qualify for like-kind exchanges or installment sales tax treatment. A dealer may be able to use these strategies under very limited circumstances. The investor/dealer label is applied to each property transaction, so individuals who are normally dealers can be investors with respect to a particular property. For example, a building used by a dealer in his trade or business may be considered an investment. Of course, someone who is normally a dealer will have a harder time proving that she is an investor.

Should the IRS challenge your claimed investor status, you have the burden of proving that you are indeed an investor. Keep good notes and records that reflect your intent at the time you purchased the property. Organizational documents for entities that hold property should reflect your investment purpose. In a partnership, for example, the partnership agreement could include an investment purpose provision. Most importantly, before you take a position on whether you are an investor or dealer, meet with a qualified tax advisor.

> **DO YOU PLAN TO SUBDIVIDE?**
>
> Section 1237 of the tax code provides that a taxpayer will not be treated as a dealer solely because he subdivided a parcel of property for sale. This section includes several qualifications that you need to go over with a tax advisor and only applies to parcels for which no more than five subdivided lots are sold.

Estimate Your Gain or Loss and Tax Liability

With these important tax concepts under review, it is time to start doing the math. Knowing your potential tax liability can be a real motivator. To estimate gain or loss and the potential tax liability on the sale of your property, follow these steps:

1. Determine the net sales proceeds.
   - Net sales proceeds are equal to the gross sales price minus the selling expenses. A rule of thumb is that the selling expenses (sometimes called cost of sales) for an investment property can run to 10 percent of the selling price. Selling expenses can include real estate commissions, attorney and accountant fees, settlement and escrow fees, title insurance, and related closing costs.
2. Determine your adjusted basis in the property.
   - The original basis of a property you buy is usually its cost; however, your basis may be something other than the cost if you if acquired it by one of the following means:
     - A gift—your basis is the carryover basis of the property from the benefactor.

- Inheritance—the basis can be the full fair market value of the property at the time the property is transferred, which could eliminate the need to pay any tax on the sale of the property.

- Like-kind exchange—the basis of the new property is the substituted basis of the exchanged property.

As discussed earlier, the cost basis is usually adjusted up or down over time for certain additions and deductions.

3. Determine the total gain or loss on the sale.
   – The total gain or loss on the sale of a real property is calculated by subtracting the adjusted basis from the net sales price.

4. Adjust the total gain, factoring in accumulated depreciation and suspended or carry-forward losses from the property.
   – If you have losses that have carried forward during your ownership, deduct them from the net sales proceeds. Suspended or carry-forward losses are those losses that you could not use in prior tax years because of limitations.

5. Determine whether you have held the property for more than one year and whether you are an investor or dealer.

Example: Say you are selling an investment property to a buyer for $500,000. Your cost to purchase the property five years ago was $300,000. At the time you sell, you have taken $28,300 in depreciation, and this depreciation is the only adjustment to your cost basis. This means your adjusted basis is $271,700. Your sale costs (commissions, title fees, attorneys' fees,) are 10 percent of the gross sales price or $50,000. Figure 1.2 shows gain on sale for this example.

Selling Price	$500,000
Less costs of sale	($50,000)
Less adjusted basis	($271,300)
Gain on sale	**$178,700**

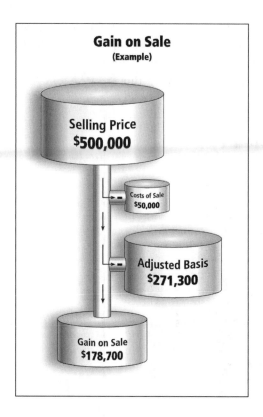

FIGURE 1.2 Gain on sale

Assuming you are an investor and have held the property for more than one year, your gain is subject to the long-term capital gain rate of 15 percent, except for the amount of depreciation taken, which will be subject to the depreciation recapture rate of 25 percent.

Long-Term Gain:		
Recognized gain	$178,700	
Less depreciation taken	$ 28,300	
		$150,400 x 15%
Tax		$22,560
PLUS		
Depreciation recapture		$28,300 x 25%
Tax		$7,075
Total federal tax liability	$29,635	

Do not forget to also take into account your state capital gain tax liability, if your state has one. The federal and state capital gains tax rate applicable to you is called your combined capital gains rate.

Figure 1.3 shows the income tax liability for this example.

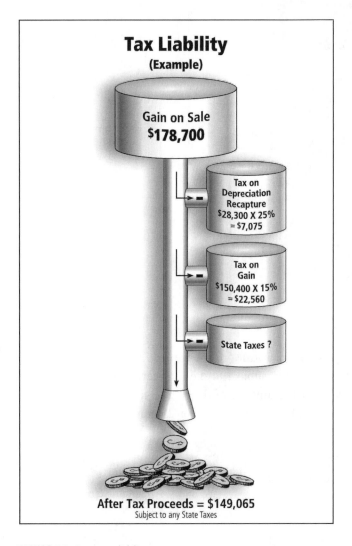

FIGURE 1.3 Income tax liability

SALES PRICE

In the previous example, the investor knew the sales price of the property. If you do not have a buyer yet and want to estimate your potential tax liability, you will need to estimate the value of the property. The most accurate estimates of value will come from a professional real estate appraiser. Although these property-specific appraisals are not free, they are worth the cost since they can be used as independent valuations for tax purposes. Appraisers traditionally use one or more of three basic valuation techniques to estimate the current value of a property: the sales comparison approach, the cost approach, and the income capitalization approach (for larger income-producing properties).

> ### BUYING INCOME
>
> When buying an income-producing property, estimate the value based on the expected income. You may also want the right to terminate the transaction if the property is not generating the expected income at the time of closing. You may even want to have the seller guarantee the level of income for a minimum period of time. If the property fails to generate the required level of income, the purchase price would be adjusted.

OUR LEGAL SYSTEM

The legal system, just like the tax system, offers several advantages to real estate owners and investors. Our laws define property rights and offer ways to protect those rights. In this section, we review the way our laws define and classify different types of property and establish how it can be owned and transferred.

Forms of Property

There are basically three forms of property related to real estate: real property, personal property, and fixtures. Separating the value of real property and fixtures from personal property is necessary for calculating things like depreciation deductions. Sometimes we refer to real estate and real property or realty, but it means the same thing—land and anything permanently attached to it. There are times when the value of real estate needs to be apportioned between the land and improvements or buildings.

In contrast, personal property is movable property. Personal property is typically without title, unlike real estate, and is transferred with a bill of sale. There is also an in-between class of property called fixtures. A fixture is a piece of personal property that is permanently attached to real property. For example, a ceiling fan starts out as personal property until it is attached to the ceiling, at which time it becomes a fixture. Once something becomes a fixture it is included as part of the real property.

Forms of Ownership

There are different forms of ownership, and each one comes with different rights and imposes different obligations on the owners. *Fee simple* is the most common way real estate is owned in the United States. It is the most complete form of ownership and is required by almost all lenders before they will loan money to purchase or improve the property. Property owned by a single individual is straightforward. If a property is owned by more than one person, then there are a few types of concurrent ownership that could apply, each with very different consequences.

Joint Tenancy

The most common type of co-ownership and the one typically used by a husband and wife when they purchase a home is called *joint tenancy with right of survivorship*, or *joint tenancy* for short. In most states, creating a joint tenancy with right of survivorship requires a specific reference in the deed; otherwise, the default will be tenancy-in-common.

With joint tenancy each joint tenant is treated as having an equal interest in the property. The right-of-survivorship feature means that if one owner dies the deceased owner's interest in the property automatically passes to the surviving owner. The result is that the deceased owner's interest in the property simply evaporates.

This automatic transfer of ownership to the surviving joint tenant(s) is significant for at least two reasons. First, the transfer cannot be changed by provisions in a will or trust. Second, the property is not subject to probate—a local court administrative process.

Tenancy in Common

Tenancy in common is most often the default form of joint owner-ship. Each owner is referred to as a tenant in common and is regarded as owning separate and distinct shares of the real property, which may differ in size. This form of ownership is often used when the owners are not married or the owners have contributed different amounts to the purchase of the property. Tenants in common have no right of survivorship. This means that if one owner dies his interest passes by inheritance either through his will or trust or by intestate succession (without a valid will or trust). If an owner wants to break the joint ownership, he must file a lawsuit to cause a partition of the property or order a sale where physical partition is not practicable.

Legal Entities

Title to real property can also be held by a corporation, partnership, limited liability company, trust, or estate. There are different tax advantages and asset protection opportunities to each of these types of entities. Chapter 10 covers how to choose an appropriate ownership structure for your real estate. Generally, limited liability companies and certain types of partnerships are the preferred entities for real estate investors.

Other Ownership Methods

Other ownership structures that deserve mention are cooperatives, condominiums, and real estate investment trust (REIT) shares. A cooperative housing corporation, or coop, is a corporate entity established to construct, maintain, and operate an apartment building for the benefit of its tenant shareholders. Each shareholder tenant has a lease with the corporation that entitles her to the exclusive use of a specific apartment. By contrast, the owner of a condominium unit owns her particular unit and has an undivided common interest in the underlying land and improvements. A variation of the condominium is the townhome. The owner of a townhome typically owns her unit and the land under it but may share a wall with another unit under a party wall agreement.

Finally, there is REIT. REITs are not going to be the vehicle of choice for most real estate investors buying specific property, so we do not discuss the details of qualifying for REIT status. While most investors are not going to start their own REIT, it is becoming popular to invest in REIT shares as a way of owning real estate, particularly expensive commercial real estate projects.

REITs are corporations, trusts, or associations that must qualify for special tax treatment. REITs normally own large income-producing properties and have many owners, and some are publicly traded. Owning a publicly traded REIT can be a great way to diversify a stock portfolio with real estate without the headaches that come with being a landlord. Plus, REITs are required to distribute 95 percent of their taxable income (not including capital gain) to their owners, so it can be a good source of income.

CLOSING NOTES

After learning the basics in this first chapter, you are ready to discover the tax and legal strategies outlined in the rest of the book. Remember, while a tax professional may file your returns, it is up to you to take action and document your activities in ways that enable you to use the best tax and legal strategies. Below is a list of things to keep in mind from this chapter as you move forward.

➤ Income and gain from real estate is preferred to wage and salary income because it is taxed at lower tax rates and there are more available deductions and exemptions.

➤ Gain from real property held for more than one year receives preferred long-term capital gain treatment.

➤ Real estate investor status is preferred to dealer status in most cases.

➤ To estimate gain or loss and potential tax liability for a property you need to estimate the value of the property and determine the property's adjusted basis.

➤ A real estate investment may contain several different forms of property that need to be classified and assigned a separate value to calculate things like depreciation and taxes.

➤ There are many different forms of ownership and ways to hold title to real property that can impact the way the property is transferred and the available tax strategies and asset protection options.

PART ONE
Keep More Income

CHAPTER 2

Maximize Home and Rental Property Write-Offs

An investment in knowledge pays the best interest.

—Benjamin Franklin

B en Franklin spoke the truth, especially if you own real estate. Knowing how to use expense and loss deductions properly can increase your after-tax return. You can even start at home, which is convenient since the first significant real estate purchase most people make is their home. After purchasing a home, many people move on to rental property. Fortunately, the Internal Revenue Code provides tax incentives to both homeowners and rental property investors. These tax benefits can enhance your return when the real estate market is good and may be your only return on investment when the real estate market is in a slump.

In this chapter, we focus on many of the expenses and deductions that make home and rental property ownership so enticing. However, if you are a real estate investor you will also need to carefully read the next chapter where we cover perhaps the most significant tax deduction—depreciation. In the next chapter, we also explain how the IRS limits the use of all deductions with the passive activity loss rules.

PRINCIPAL RESIDENCE EXPENSES AND DEDUCTIONS

In this section, we outline some the most commonly used expenses and deductions available to homeowners, including home mortgage interest, points, and home office expenses. We also discuss the difference between making improvements and repairs to your home and what that means to your bottom line.

Deducting Mortgage Interest

One of the biggest reoccurring tax advantages of owning a home is the ability to reduce annual income taxes by deducting home mortgage interest payments. Generally, home mortgage interest is any interest you pay on a loan secured by your principal residence or a second home. Home mortgage interest can come from a home purchase mortgage, a second mortgage, a home equity loan, or a line of credit as long as it meets certain tests. Home mortgage interest specifically excludes interest paid on personal loans. Personal loans include things like automobile financing and credit cards.

The initial tests you must pass in order to be able to deduct home mortgage interest are:

➤ You must file Form 1040 and itemize deductions on Schedule A;
➤ You must be legally liable for the loan; and
➤ The mortgage must be a secured debt on a qualified home.

Form 1040 is the U.S. Individual Income Tax Return. Schedule A is for taxpayers who itemize their deductions rather than take the standard deduction.

As the rule says, you must be legally liable for the loan. You cannot deduct interest payments you make for someone else (like a family member) unless you are legally liable to make them. In addition, the loan must be a bona fide debt that is intended to be repaid, and it must be secured by a qualified home in which the taxpayer has an interest.

A qualified home can be a house, cooperative apartment, condominium, mobile home, house boat, or any other property that has basic living accommodations such as a sleeping space, a toilet, and cooking facilities. If you are building a home, you may treat it as a qualified home for up to twenty-four months provided it becomes a qualified home when it is ready to be occupied.

Next, repayment of the loan must be secured by the qualified home. To be secured, the taxpayer must have signed a legal document, typically a mortgage or deed of trust, that: (1) makes the home security for repayment on the loan, (2) provides that the taxpayer's home could be used to pay off the debt in the event of default, and (3) is recorded or otherwise perfected based on local and state law.

HOME MORTGAGE INTEREST VERSUS PERSONAL LOAN INTEREST

The possibility of interest deductions, and lower interest rates, are why many advisors recommend paying off nondeductible interest on automobile loans and credit card debt with a home equity loan.

If these tests are satisfied, most people are able to deduct the full amount of all of their home interest payments; however, there are limitations. Your home mortgage interest deduction is limited to the total of the:

1. Maximum allowable home acquisition debt;
2. Maximum allowable home equity debt; and
3. Grandfathered debt.

Home acquisition debt is a loan secured by a qualified home, taken out after October 13, 1987, and used to buy, build, or substantially improve the qualified home. Only debt that does not exceed the cost of the home plus improvements can be home acquisition debt. The maximum home acquisition debt allowed (including your primary home and a second home) is $1 million ($500,000 if married and filing separately). This limit is reduced by grandfathered debt, which we will explain later. Plus, if you have excess home acquisition debt you still may be able to deduct some or all of your interest payments if it qualifies as home equity debt.

Home equity debt is a loan taken out after October 13, 1987 that does not qualify as home acquisition debt or as grandfathered debt and is secured by your qualified home. Excess home acquisition debt and loans used for purposes other than buying, building, or substantially improving a home may qualify as home equity debt. Home equity debt (on your primary home and second home) is limited to the smaller of $100,000

FAMILY LOANS

Interest paid to a family member through an intra-family loan is deductible as long as the loan arrangement reflects a true debtor-creditor relationship and the amount of interest paid can be definitely determined. Keep clear records of the loan payments and separate out the portion attributable to interest, just like a commercial lender.

($50,000 if married and filing separately) and the total of each home's fair market value minus home acquisition and grandfathered debt.

Finally, grandfathered debt is debt on your home taken out before October 14, 1987. It also includes refinancing of those loans to the extent the refinanced debt does not exceed the principal balance on the original debt. To the extent it does exceed the principal balance, it could still be home acquisition or home equity debt. Grandfathered debt is not limited. All interest you pay on grandfathered debt is fully deductible home mortgage interest. However, grandfathered debt reduces your $1 million home acquisition debt and potentially the limit for your home equity debt.

Deducting Mortgage Points

Another potentially valuable deduction is the points paid in obtaining a home mortgage. A point is a fee paid by a borrower. Points are also known as loan origination fees, loan discount points, or just discount points. Points are usually expressed as a percentage of the loan. For example, 2 points means 2 percent of the loan balance. Generally, you cannot deduct the full amount of points in the year paid. Points are typically considered prepaid interest and must be deducted over the term of the loan.

Not surprisingly, there is an exception. Those who buy or build their primary home and meet the following tests can fully deduct the points in the year paid:

1. The loan is secured by your main home.
2. Paying points is an established business practice in the area where the loan was made.

3. The points paid were not more than points generally charged in the area where the loan was made.

4. The points paid were not paid in place of amounts that ordinarily are stated separately on the settlement statement, such as appraisal and inspection fees.

5. The funds you provide (other than those borrowed from the lender or mortgage broker), plus any points the seller paid, must be at least as much as the points charged.

> **WHAT DO YOU DO IF YOUR MORTGAGE IS ABOVE THE LIMITS**
>
> You may consider selling or cashing out some of your other investments to pay down your home mortgage in order to meet the qualified mortgage limitations.

6. The loan is used to buy or build your main home.

7. The points were computed as a percentage of the principal amount of the mortgage.

8. The amount is clearly shown on the settlement statement.

Points paid on home improvement loans for your main home can also be fully deducted in the year paid if tests 1–5 are met. However, points paid on loans secured by a second home cannot be fully deducted in the year paid. Points for second homes must be amortized over the life of the loan. Similarly, points paid to refinance a mortgage must usually be amortized over the life of the loan. If tests 1–5 are met and part of the refinance proceeds are used for improvements to your main home, then you may be able to fully deduct the portion of the points related to the improvement in the year paid.

If you do not qualify or do not choose to deduct the points in the year paid, then you can deduct them equally over the life of the loan provided you meet all of the following tests:

1. The loan is secured by a home.

2. The loan period is not longer than thirty years.

3. If the loan period is longer than ten years, the terms of your loan are the same as other loans offered in your area for the same or longer period.

4. Either the loan amount is $250,000 or less or the number of points is not more than 4 for loan periods of fifteen years or less or 6 for loan periods of more than fifteen years.

Note that points paid by the seller in connection with the buyer's home mortgage loan are considered points paid by the buyer. In addition, the buyer's basis in the home is reduced by the amount of the points paid by the seller.

Deducting Home Office Expenses

The Internet and computers have enabled a large work-at-home work force. Many people work at home in some capacity. Just because you check your email after dinner does not mean you can (or should) start deducting expenses associated with the business use of part of your home.

The IRS starts from the premise that homeowners cannot deduct expenses such as mortgage interest and real estate taxes as business expenses. However, if you can meet certain strict tests, you may be able to qualify for certain exceptions and deduct some expenses related to the business use of part of your home. To qualify to deduct expenses for the business use of your home, you must use part of your home:

➤ Regularly and exclusively as your principal place of business; or
➤ Regularly and exclusively as a place to meet or deal with your patients, clients, or customers in the normal course of your trade or business; or
➤ In the case of a separate structure not attached to your home, in connection with your business; or
➤ On a regular basis for certain storage use; or
➤ For rental use; or
➤ As a daycare facility.

If you are an employee you must also meet the following two requirements: your business use must be for the convenience of your employer (just helpful is not enough), and you must not rent any part or your home to your employer and use the rented portion to perform services as an employee for that employer.

These rules are not as easy to follow as they sound. To qualify for exclusive use you must use a specific area of your home only for your trade or business. You do not meet this test if you use the area for both business and personal purposes. For example, a consultant using his spare bedroom to check e-mails and write reports does not cut it if the bedroom is also frequently used by visiting guests and family. The consultant cannot claim a deduction for the business use of the spare bedroom because it is not used exclusively for his consultancy work.

WATCH OUT!

Claiming a home office deduction is a common trigger for an IRS audit given the number of abuses in this area. If you plan to claim a deduction for business use of your home, make sure you meet the strict requirements.

To meet the regular use test, the taxpayer must use the specific area for business on a regular basis. Incidental or occasional use is not regular use. Logging a few hours on the weekend or checking e-mail in the evenings is not likely to be considered regular use.

Also, remember that this deduction is limited to trade or business use. Reading financial reports and conducting online research for your investment portfolio is probably a profit-seeking activity, not a trade or business.

If you are claiming that you use part of your home as a principal place of business, then you must show you use your home office or work area:

➤ Exclusively and regularly for administrative or management activities of your trade or business; and
➤ Have no other fixed location where you conduct substantial administrative or management activities of your trade or business.

It may be easier to show that you use an area of your home exclusively to meet with patients, clients, or customers in the normal course of your business. For example, a self-employed consultant working three days a week in her city office and two days a week in her home office may qualify if she regularly meets with clients at her home office.

If you use part of your home regularly and exclusively for a trade or business, you can be eligible to take some valuable deductions. First, you

PRINCIPAL RESIDENCE EXCLUSION

If you sell your home, the gain on the part of your house used for business and depreciated will not be covered by the principal residence exclusion and could result in taxable gain and depreciation recapture.

will need to divide qualifying home expenses between personal use and business use. This division can be based on area, time usage, or any other reasonable method. Expenses that may be divided include real estate taxes, deductible mortgage interest, utilities and services, insurance, and repairs. In addition to these expenses, you may depreciate the part of your home used for business as non-residential real property using the straight-line method over thirty-nine years.

Attributing part of your home mortgage interest, property taxes, and other home expenses to business expenses may be particularly beneficial for those with higher incomes who cannot claim itemized deductions on Schedule A. Remember from the discussion of mortgage interest and points that in order to claim the deduction you must file Form 1040 and itemize deductions on Schedule A. The home office deduction allows you to deduct a portion of the mortgage interest, property taxes, and other home expenses on a separate business schedule.

Home Improvements and Repairs

Even though home repairs are necessary, they are not beneficial from a tax standpoint. Home repairs are considered personal expenses; they are not deductible and cannot be added to the home's basis. An improvement, however, adds to the value of the home and its basis. Therefore, it is best to make improvements, not repairs, to your home. The opposite is true for rental properties, which are discussed below.

How does an improvement differ from a repair? An improvement adds to the value of your home, prolongs its useful life, or adapts it to new uses. Repairs, on the other hand, maintain your home in good condition. For example, putting up a new roof is an improvement whereas replacing a few damaged shingles is a repair.

Improvements can be big or small. Adding a room to your house is an obvious improvement; however, built-in appliances and fixtures can also be considered improvements. Other improvements include constructing built-in bookcases and adding new light fixtures. Land-scaping, such as planting trees and shrubs, may also qualify as an improvement under the right circumstances. Grading the lot to ease access to the property is more likely to be an improvement than decorative landscaping.

RENTAL PROPERTY EXPENSES AND DEDUCTIONS

As we mentioned at the beginning of this chapter, the tax code also provides some great tax advantages to rental property investors. One primary goal of most rental property investors is to create rent income. Generally, rent income is included in your gross income. Rental income includes the actual rent payments plus: (1) any expenses of the investor paid by a tenant, (2) the fair market value of services provided in lieu of rent, (3) payments by a tenant for cancelling a lease, and (4) payments by tenant for an option to purchase the property.

One of the few times rent is not included in income is when you rent property that you also use as your home or second home and you rent it for fourteen days or less during the year. The property is primarily used as a home, not a rental. That means you are also not permitted to deduct rental expenses.

In the subsections that follow we discuss expenses and deductions that can reduce taxable rental income. Most of the ordinary and necessary expenses of renting a property can be deducted from its rental income. Generally, rental expenses are deducted in the year you pay them. And they can be deducted even if the property is vacant as long as it is held out for rent.

Repairs and Improvements

Rental properties require maintenance. Sometimes this means repairing broken windows or fixing leaks. Other times it means improving the property by installing a new water heater or modernizing the kitchen. Whether you make a repair or an improvement impacts how much you can deduct. Repairs are preferred with rental properties because the entire expense is deductable in the year it is paid. Improvements, on the other hand, are considered capital assets and must be depreciated over time.

Repairs differ from improvements in that repairs keep the property in good operating condition but do not materially add to the value of the property or substantially extend the life of the property. If a repair is part of an extensive remodeling or restoration of the property, then it must be included in the whole job and treated as an improvement instead of a repair. Here are a few things to keep in mind to maximize your deductions for repairs:

➤ Schedule and track repairs and improvements separately;
➤ Use comparable materials when making repairs since using better materials may seem more like an improvement;
➤ Limit repairs to damaged areas only; and
➤ Make repairs following a triggering event, such as a broken water pipe.

Also, be sure to keep accurate records. To keep repair work separate from improvement work you may want to arrange for the work to be done at different times and by different contractors if possible. For improvements, you will need to know the cost of improvements when you sell or depreciate your rental property.

Other Expenses

There are many other expenses that can be deducted from rental income as well as the cost of repairs. Some of these expenses include advertising, cleaning and maintenance, utilities, insurance, taxes, mortgage interest, points, commissions, tax return preparation fees, certain travel and transportation expenses, and rental payments for equipment or leasehold interests.

If you rent a condominium or cooperative apartment, you may also deduct dues or assessments for care of the common areas as long as the funds are used for maintenance and not improvements or capital assets.

If you rent part of your property and use another part for personal use, then you must divide certain expenses between the two parts as though they were separate properties. For example, painting the exterior of a home would normally be a nondeductible personal expense, but if you rent a room in the home you may use a reasonable method of dividing the expense and deduct a part of the cost as a rental expense. You do not have to divide expenses that belong only to the rental part of the property. For example, the entire cost of painting a room that you rent is a rental expense.

Similarly if you have a vacation home that you rent, you must divide your expenses between rental use and personal use. If you used your vacation home as a home, you cannot deduct rental expenses that are more than your rental income for the property. Whether the IRS will consider the property used as a home is discussed in detail in Chapter 4. If the property is not used as a home, you can deduct rental expenses that are more than your rental income, subject to certain limitations we discuss in the next chapter.

CLOSING NOTES

The Internal Revenue Code provides basic expense and deduction strategies to decrease taxes for homeowners and rental property investors. Knowing how to maximize these expense and loss deductions can increase your after-tax return. The deductions in this chapter can be valuable; however, you will need to read the next chapter to learn about the ultimate rental property deduction—depreciation. In the next chapter, we also outline the passive activity loss limitations that apply when your rental expenses exceed your rental income. A few more notes to close this chapter are listed below.

➤ Homeowners can deduct qualifying home mortgage interest on their principal home and a second home. The deductible mortgage interest must be related to acquisition indebtedness and is limited to $1 million of debt ($500,000 for a married individual filing a separate tax return).

➤ Interest paid on qualifying home equity loans can also be deducted up to a limit of the lesser of $100,000 ($50,000 for a married person filing a separate tax return) and the difference between the fair market value of the property and the total acquisition debt.

➤ Points paid to obtain a home mortgage loan on a primary home may also be deductible.

➤ Interest from personal debt like credit cards and automobile loans is not deductable. Consider refinancing such debt into a home equity loan.

➤ Unlike a rental property, repairs to a principal residence are personal expenses and are not deductable, but improvements are added to your basis and can therefore help your tax position when you sell.

➤ Homeowners can also deduct qualifying business expenses associated with the business use of part of their home, but use caution here. Home office deductions have been known to trigger IRS audits, and the requirements to take this deduction are strict.

➤ Rental property owners should make repairs rather than improvements when possible. Repairs are deducted in the year made while improvements must be depreciated over many years.

CHAPTER 3

Depreciation Deductions and Loss Limitations

If you would be wealthy, think of saving as well as getting.

—Benjamin Franklin

A dollar saved with smart tax planning is worth more than a taxable dollar earned. This basic economic logic is why the strategies in this book are so useful for building wealth. In this chapter, we cover one of the best deduction strategies available to real estate investors—the depreciation deduction. The depreciation deduction can save you income taxes without reducing your cash flow! Of course, like most tax benefits, depreciation deductions have rules and limits you need to know. The limits that impact depreciation deductions are commonly referred to as the passive activity loss limitations and also can limit the use of other expenses, deductions, and losses we discuss in this book. In the second half of this chapter we cover the passive activity loss limitations.

THE PHANTOM EXPENSE

Depreciation is an annual income tax deduction that reflects the cost of an asset or its reduction in value due to wear and tear over the course of its useful life. An asset's useful life is the time frame in which the IRS requires the cost of the asset to be recovered. The cost of an asset with a useful life of less than one year is written off or expensed in the fiscal year in which it was purchased. Unlike ordinary expenses such as insurance, utilities, or maintenance, with depreciation you do not pay anything out of pocket for this cost, yet you can use it to reduce your taxable income. For this reason depreciation is sometimes referred to as a phantom expense or accounting fiction.

The idea is simple enough to understand with an asset like a dump truck used in a construction business. A dump truck decreases in value each year it is used in the business and can be expected to last about five years before it needs to be replaced. Real estate, at least historically, does not lose value but rather appreciates in value over time despite wear and tear. This is the greatness of real property depreciation; the IRS allows (in fact, requires) you to depreciate the property even if the value of the property has increased and you have a positive cash flow from rental income.

> *Example:* An investor buys a four-unit apartment building for $500,000.
> He put $100,000 down and financed the remainder. His $400,000 loan
> has a 7 percent interest rate that costs about $2,662 per month. Repairs,
> insurance, marketing, and management fees are an additional $500 per
> month. The monthly rental is $1,000 per unit or $4,000 per month for
> the fully leased building. That works out to a positive monthly cash flow
> (income less expenses) of $838 per month or $10,056 per year. Assuming
> a 30 percent marginal tax rate, that means the investor would pay about
> $3,000 in federal taxes.

The depreciation deduction dramatically changes his tax scenario. The investor divides the cost of the building (we will assume that building accounts for $425,000 of the purchase price) by the recovery period of twenty-seven and a half years for a residential rental property to get an annual depreciation deduction of $15,454. He has completely eliminated his federal taxes on the $10,056 of rental income and generated a loss! You may be wondering what happens to the remaining $5,398 in excess depreciation. Subject to the at-risk rules and passive activity limits discussed later in the chapter, it may be possible to apply this loss to income from other sources. Figure 3.1 shows how the depreciation deductions works.

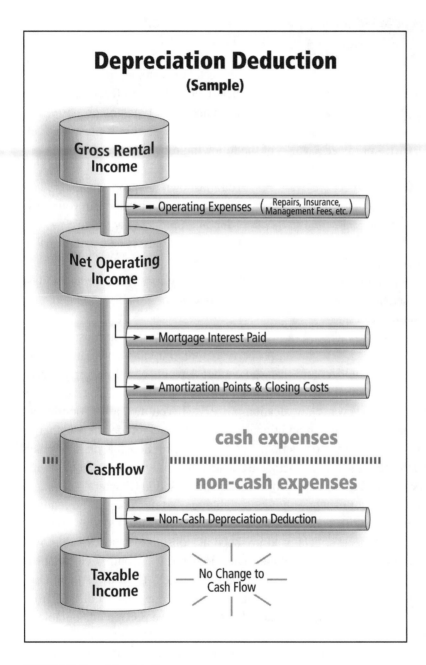

FIGURE 3.1 Depreciation deduction

IMPROVEMENTS VERSUS LAND

A good (and defensible) method of allocating your purchase price between land and improvements or buildings is to examine the county tax assessments for the property. The actual dollar amounts may be significantly less than your purchase price due to the nature of county assessments, but the proportion allocated to land and improvements provides a good rule of thumb for depreciation calculations.

WHAT PROPERTY CAN BE DEPRECIATED?

Most real estate investment property can be depreciated, but there are a few requirements that eliminate some types of property. For property to be depreciable it must meet all of the following requirements:

➤   You must own the property;
➤   You must use the property in your business or income-producing activities;
➤   The property must have a determinable useful life; and
➤   The property must be expected to last more than one year.

It is no surprise that you must own the property before you can depreciate it. And most people understand that you cannot depreciate real property that is held for personal use, such as your primary residence. There is often a question, however, with vacation property. If you own a vacation home, you need to engage in additional planning before you decide whether to take a depreciation deduction. The tax treatment depends on how much the property is used for personal use and how often it is rented to others. The nuances of vacation properties are discussed in Chapter 4.

The major exception to depreciable real estate is land. The requirement of having a determinable useful life means that the property wears out, decays, gets used up, becomes obsolete, or loses value over a period of time. Undeveloped land does not wear out, become obsolete, or get used up, so it cannot be depreciated. If an investment contains land and improvements, you need to separate the cost of land from the cost of improvements and only depreciate the portion attributable to improvements.

The determinable useful life requirement can be a concern in drafting leases. If not properly drafted, a lease can take away a property owner's right to depreciation. Most leases contain a provision requiring the tenant to maintain the property in good condition, subject to normal wear and tear. If the tenant has to return the property in exactly the same condition, including repairing or replacing damage through normal wear and tear, then it can be argued the property is not losing value or depreciating. The owner should not be able to recover his capital costs through depreciation if the tenant carries all of this responsibility.

HOW MUCH CAN BE DEPRECIATED?

The IRS provides specific rules and schedules to help you figure the amount of deduction for different types of assets. For rental property, there are three methods that can be used to calculate depreciation depending on the type of property and when you placed it in service.

➤ MACRS (Modified Accelerated Cost Recovery System) for property placed in service after 1986.
➤ ACRS (Accelerated Cost Recovery System) for property placed in service after 1980 but before 1987.
➤ Useful lives and either straight-line or an accelerated method of depreciation, such as the declining balance method, for property placed in service before 1981.

MACRS is the most common method for business or investment property placed in service after 1986. To figure your depreciation deduction for a property using MACRS you need to know:

1. The property's recovery period;
2. The date the property was placed in service; and
3. The property's depreciable basis.

Recovery Period: The IRS assigns a recovery period to each class of property that can be depreciated. The recovery period for residential rental property is twenty-seven and a half years. The class for residential rental property includes real property that is a rental building or

SEPARATE YOUR RENTAL ACTIVITY ASSETS INTO CLASSES

Rental activities may contain several property classes, and you need to separate out the costs of each class before taking depreciation. Capital assets such as appliances and furniture have a different recovery period than the building. The building includes components such as furnaces, water pipes, and vents. Properly allocate cost to nondepreciable land, buildings or improvements, and other items such as furniture and appliances for maximum depreciation.

structure for which 80 percent or more of the gross rental income for the tax year is from the dwelling units. The recovery period for nonresidential real property (another way to say commercial real property) is thirty-nine years.

Placed-in-Service Date: The date you acquire residential rental property is not necessarily the date you can begin taking depreciation. You must wait until the date you place the property in service to start taking depreciation. Placing a rental property in service means the date on which the property is ready and available for rent. For example, if you bought a rental property on December 2 of last year, made repairs to the property, and had it ready for rent on May 15 of the following year, then it would be considered placed in service in June and you could start taking depreciation deductions.

Depreciable Basis: Finally, you need to determine the property's depreciable basis. For rental property, this is its cost or other basis when you acquired it, adjusted up or down for certain changes that occur before you place the property in service. The cost basis is the amount you paid for the property in cash, in debt obligations, or in other property or services, and it also includes certain settlement fees and other closing costs. The basis may be increased by items such as additions or improvements having a useful life of more than one year and may be decreased by items such as proceeds from insurance as a result of casualty or theft. Depreciable additions or improvements made after you place the property in service must be accounted for separately.

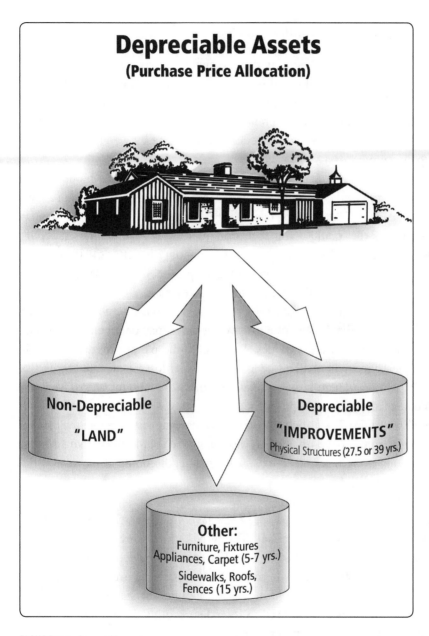

FIGURE 3.2 Depreciable assets

PASSIVE ACTIVITY LOSS RULES

The example at the beginning of the chapter raised an interesting question: What happens if you do not have enough rental income to take full advantage of the depreciation deduction? The investor in the example had positive cash flow from rental income but it was less than his annual depreciation, so once the deduction was made he showed a loss (referred to as a *paper loss*).

Prior to 1986, you could reduce your taxable income by deducting losses from real estate investments. Many people, especially those with high salaries, like doctors, became real estate investors simply to generate losses that could offset their non–real estate income. The rationale behind the post-1986 rules is that the economy is better off if investors are focused on an investment's inherent profitability instead of just the tax savings to be achieved through the investment.

Rental real estate is generally considered a passive activity, and the gist of the rule is that losses from passive activities may only be used to offset income from passive activities. We discuss the passive loss rules in this chapter since many real estate losses are paper losses generated by excess depreciation. There are two rules that limit the amount of loss you can deduct from an income-producing activity: the at-risk rules and the passive activity limits. The at-risk rules are applied to any losses before the passive activity rules, so we will start by discussing the at-risk rules. Like all rules, there are a couple of exceptions, so do not get discouraged.

At-Risk Rules

The at-risk rules are a set of tax laws that limit the amount of tax losses an investor can deduct. The at-risk rules were extended to real estate investments in 1986 and apply to property placed in service after 1986. Essentially, losses on real estate investments are deductible only to the extent of the amount of money the investor stands to lose or the capital the investor has at risk. When determining the amount of capital at risk, the following amounts can be included:

➤ Cash contributed to the real estate activity;
➤ The adjusted tax basis of other property contributed to the activity;

➤ Borrowed money for which the investor is personally liable or has pledged other property as security for the real estate activity; and

➤ Borrowed money for which the investor is not personally liable, provided these nonrecourse loans meet certain conditions.

For example, if you have $50,000 at risk in a real estate investment that generates $10,000 in rental income per year, then the losses may only be claimed as deductions for five years despite the property's much longer useful life. You will need to contribute more money or property or take on more qualifying debt in order to deduct losses beyond the fifth year.

Passive Activity Limits

Once you determine the amount of capital you have at risk, the next step is to apply the limits on passive activity losses. You can generally only use losses from passive activities to offset income from passive activities. Rental activities are treated as passive activities, unless you qualify as a real estate professional. So what exactly is a rental activity? Anytime real or personal property is used or held for use by customers and the gross income from the activity represents the amount paid mainly for the use of the property you have rental activity. Examples of rental activity include:

➤ Leased residential property

➤ Leased vacation homes if the average rental period is more than seven days

➤ Leased condos if the average rental period is more than seven days

➤ Leased commercial buildings

➤ Leased land

➤ Mini-warehouses

➤ Self-storage units

It does not matter whether the use is under a lease, a service contract, or some other arrangement. Activities may be excluded from the definition of a rental activity under the following scenarios:

1. The average rental period is seven days or less. Examples: short-term use of condominiums and hotel or motel rooms.
2. The average rental period is thirty days or less and significant personal services are provided with the rental. Examples: hotels, resorts, and spas.
3. Extraordinary personal services are included with the rental. Examples: nursing homes and boarding schools.
4. The rental is incidental to nonrental activity. This generally applies if the main purpose of holding the property is for investment or business and the rental income is not significant, for the convenience of the taxpayer and his employees, or held for sale to customers.
5. The rental property is available during defined business hours for nonexclusive use by customers. Examples: a golf course or spa.
6. The property is used in a nonrental activity of a partnership, S corporation, or joint venture in which the taxpayer has an interest. (This is designed to prevent taxpayers from converting active income to passive income by renting to entities in which they have an interest.)
7. The property includes nondepreciable property, such as vacant land, and less than 30 percent of the property's basis is nondepreciable.

If an activity is not a rental activity, net losses are considered passive and still subject to the passive limitations unless the taxpayer materially participates in the business activity. If the activity is a rental activity, then losses are considered passive even if you materially participate unless you materially participate as a real estate professional. Before discussing the requirements for being a real estate professional, first let's look at a special $25,000 rental allowance that can allow you to offset up to $25,000 of nonpassive income with passive losses.

The $25,000 Rental Allowance or Active Participation Exception

There is a special allowance that allows you to deduct up to $25,000 of real estate losses from nonpassive income such as wages, interest, and dividends. This special allowance is for individuals (not corporations) who actively participate in passive rental real estate activity. To qualify for this special allowance, you must:

➤ Have a modified adjusted gross income of less than $150,000;
➤ Actively participate in the activity;
➤ Own at least 10 percent (by value) of all interests in the activity; and
➤ Not be a limited partner.

The full $25,000 allowance is available to taxpayers whose adjusted gross income (AGI) is less than $100,000. For every $2 that AGI exceeds $100,000 the allowance is reduced by $1. For example, if your AGI is $110,000, then your maximum allowance is $20,000. If your AGI exceeds $150,000, you are out of luck, at least for this special allowance.

The standard for actively participating in a real estate activity is not very stringent and includes making significant management decisions. While there is not a specific hour requirement for time spent on the activity, the key is that the taxpayer use independent judgment when making decisions and not simply ratify a manager's decisions. Independent judgments can include approving tenants, leases, and repairs, even if someone else performs a majority of the work.

Exception for Real Estate Professionals

There is a major exception to the passive activity rules that allows those who qualify to deduct all of their losses from real estate. This exception is for real estate professionals. The rationale is that if a person's primary business and source of income is tied to her real estate activities, then these activities require continuing effort and are not passive. To qualify as a real estate professional for a given tax year, you must meet both of the following requirements:

➤ More than 50 percent of the personal services you performed in all trades or businesses during the tax year were performed in real property trades or businesses in which you materially participated; and
➤ You performed more than 750 hours of services during the tax year in real property trades or businesses in which you materially participated.

A real property trade or business is a trade or business that develops or redevelops, constructs or reconstructs, acquires or converts, rents or leases, operates or manages, or brokers real property. You materially participate in a real property trade or business if you are involved in its operations on a regular, continuous, and substantial basis during the year. Being an employee of a real property trade or business does not count unless you own more than 5 percent of your employer's outstanding stock or capital or profit interests.

The material participation requirement applies separately to each rental activity. In other words, you must materially participate in each rental activity for the loss to be deductible. You may, however, file a written election to group all rental real estate activities as one activity. If you do not materially participate in the activity, then the rental is treated as a passive activity despite the fact that you are a real estate professional.

Material Participation

The material participation standard is much more demanding than the active participation standard. You are deemed to have materially participated in a trade or business activity for a tax year if you meet any one of the following tests.

1. You spent more than 500 hours participating in the activity.
2. Your participation was substantially all the participation in the activity of all individuals for the tax year, including the participation of individuals who did not own any interest in the activity.
3. You participated at least as much as any other individual for the tax year, including individuals who did not own an interest in the activity, and you participated more than 100 hours.
4. The activity is a significant participant activity and you participated in all significant participation activities for more than 500 hours. A significant participation activity is any trade or business activity in which you participated for more than 100 hours during the year and in which you did not materially participate under any of the material participation tests other than this test.
5. You materially participated for any five of the ten immediately preceding tax years.

6. The activity is a personal service activity in which you materially participated for any three of the preceding tax years. An activity is a personal service activity if it involved the performance of personal services in the fields of health, law, engineering, architecture, accounting, actuarial, science, performing arts, consulting, or any other trade or business in which capital is not a material income-producing factor.

> **DOCUMENT YOUR ACTIVITIES**
>
> Keep good records so that you can substantiate your participation. You can show services performed and time spent on an activity with a calendar, daily planner, or summary of activities and time spent.

7. During the tax year you participated in the activity on a regular, continuous, and substantial basis. If you materially participated for less than 100 hours during the year you cannot meet the test.

You cannot include time spent on management of the activity if any other person received compensation for managing the activity or any other person spent more hours during the year managing the activity than you did (regardless of whether the person was compensated). This is one of the drawbacks to being a real estate professional: you may be restricted in your ability to use an outside property management company.

In general, just about any work you do in connection with the activity will count toward participation unless the work is not customary for an owner or one of your primary reasons for doing the work is to preserve your status under the passive activity rules.

You also cannot count time spent reviewing financial statements, preparing analysis, or monitoring finances or operations unless you are directly involved with the day-to-day operations of the activity. This rule essentially disqualifies time you spend on investor-related activities.

There are often questions about whether participation by spouses and corporate entities counts. Unlike the active participation rules, you can include your spouse's participation toward qualifying for material participation, even if your spouse does not own an interest in the property. In most cases, limited partners in a partnership cannot be deemed to have materially participated in an activity given their limited role in managing the business, but it is possible for them to satisfy tests 1, 5, or 6 and still qualify as a limited partner. If the taxpayer is a closely held corporation, the corporation can be treated as materially participating in the activity only if one or more shareholders holding more than 50 percent by value of the outstanding stock of the corporation materially participates in the activity.

Carrying Forward Unused Losses (Suspended Losses)

Qualifying for exceptions that allow you to apply passive real estate losses to nonpassive income can be tricky. The good news is that if you have passive losses and do not qualify for either the active participation exception or the real estate professional exception, you can carry your passive losses forward to future years. These unused losses are sometimes referred to as *suspended losses*, and they can be carried forward indefinitely until you can use them. You can use them the next time you have net passive income or when you dispose of the passive interest in a taxable transaction. In most cases, the loss will be carried forward and taken in the year the property is sold.

If you will not be able to use future losses, here is another strategy to consider. There is an alternative depreciation system under which you can make an annual election to recover the cost of real property over a forty-year period. A forty-year recovery period is longer than the standard recovery period, which means your annual depreciation deduction will be smaller and therefore any annual loss will also be smaller. This can be particularly beneficial in avoiding a buildup of suspended losses if you are not in a real estate–related business and do not have income from other passive activities.

WATCH OUT FOR RECAPTURE

While the depreciation deduction allows you to recover costs and reduce your income for a given tax year, when the property is sold the deductions will be recaptured and taxed. Remember from Chapter 1 that capital gain is the difference between the net sales price and the adjusted basis. Taking depreciation deductions reduces your adjusted basis. Over several years this can significantly reduce the adjusted basis of the property, which means more gain. That might not be so bad if the entire amount of gain was taxed at a 15 percent capital gain rate, but the portion attributable to recapture of real property depreciation is taxed at the substantially higher rate of 25 percent. Since taking depreciation is required by the IRS, there is no way to avoid its recapture in a taxable transaction.

> **SALES TO RELATED PARTIES**
>
> If you sell or transfer real property with passive losses to a related party (basically, any family member or descendant), suspended losses cannot be deducted until that person sells or transfers the property to an unrelated party.

Because there is no way to avoid recapture of depreciation on a taxable transaction and it is taxed at a high rate, it is critical to factor it into your investment analysis and strategy planning. Imagine a scenario where you have been depreciating a property for ten years but due to a downturn in the market you are not able to sell it for much more than your purchase price. You may not have any profit, but you will still have to pay a tax bill on the recapture of depreciation. There is one strategy for avoiding depreciation recapture: exchange the property in a qualifying like-kind exchange (covered in Chapter 7) where the basis (and depreciation) will be carried over to the next property and there is no realization event to trigger capital gains tax.

CLOSING NOTES ON DEPRECIATION

The depreciation deduction is an especially effective tax tool for real estate investors. This is because it is not an out-of-pocket cost like other property expenses, such as utilities, insurance, and management. To make it even better, even though real property normally appreciates, the depreciation deduction does not depend on actual depreciation. There are some limits, however. Only part of the value of most real estate can be depreciated because land is typically part of the value of a property and it is a nondepreciable asset since it does not wear out. Ultimately, the amount of the depreciation deduction you can take depends on the at-risk rules and passive activity loss limitations. A few more notes to close this chapter are listed on the next page.

➤ When calculating depreciation, the IRS establishes the useful life (or recovery period) for different asset classes. The recovery period for residential rental property is twenty-seven and a half years, and nonresidential real property is thirty-nine years.

➤ Real property depreciation can significantly reduce your taxable income for a given year, but it will be recaptured and taxed at 25 percent when you sell the property in a taxable transaction, so plan accordingly. You may be able to avoid recapture by completing a like-kind exchange.

➤ The passive activity loss limitations apply to depreciation deductions and most of the other expenses, deductions, and losses we cover in this book. First, losses on real estate investments are deductable only to the extent of the amount of money and capital an investor has at risk. Second, generally you can only offset passive income with passive losses.

➤ Typical rental activity income and losses are passive.

➤ A major exception to the passive activity loss limitations is for real estate professionals who materially participate in real estate activities. These professionals can write off an unlimited amount of losses from real estate investments against any type of wages or income.

➤ Another exception to the passive activity loss limitations is for taxpayers who actively participate (a much lower standard than materially participate) in rental activities and have an annual adjusted gross income of $150,000 or less. These taxpayers may be able to deduct up to $25,000 in passive losses from depreciation or other deductions from ordinary nonrental income each year.

➤ To the extent you cannot use losses from depreciation or other deductions because you do not have enough passive income or do not qualify for any exceptions in a particular year, you can carry forward these losses to future years when you have net passive income or when you sell the passive activity property.

CHAPTER 4

Make the Best Use of a Vacation Home

Knowing who will want to rent your vacation home and then buying based on their demands, rather than just your own family's demands, will make it much easier in the long haul when you want to rent that property out.

—Christine Karpinski, author of *How to Rent Vacation Properties*

Ms. Karpinski's advice is insightful, especially if you are buying a vacation home primarily with an investment motive; however, the principal motive of many vacation homeowners is, not surprisingly, vacation. Regardless of motive, vacation home ownership is on the rise. According to the National Association of Realtors, vacation home sales rose 4.7 percent to a record 1.07 million in 2006. To many investors a vacation home is the perfect combination of vacation, investment, and even potential retirement home.

No matter whether you are making a lifestyle purchase or diversifying your investment portfolio, it is how you use your vacation home that determines the tax strategies that are available to you. In this chapter, we cover the tax-saving strategies available to vacation home owners. We also cover special rules that apply to time-shares and fractional ownership interests.

HOME OR RENTAL PROPERTY?

A vacation home or second home is a property that may be used both personally and as a rental. The tax rules that apply to these mixed-use properties are based on how you use the property at the time of a taxable event. From a tax planning standpoint there are basically three different ways to use such a property, and each has different tax consequences. They are:

➤ Exclusive personal use
➤ Exclusive rental use
➤ Mixed personal use and rental use

Exclusive Personal Use

Sometimes a vacation property is used exclusively by the owner. This option provides the most flexibility for scheduling personal use and the least hassle since there are no renter issues. However, it also requires the most cash because the owner has no rental income to cover ownership expenses. Plus, as a true second home, the owner cannot take deductions as though the property were a rental.

It is not all bad news; however, there are still tax saving opportunities. For example, you may still be able to deduct qualified mortgage interest and real estate taxes on your second home. The qualified mortgage interest deduction is available only for your personal residence and one designated second home. So if you own a cabin at the lake and a ski condo in addition to your home, the mortgage interest on the third property will not be deductible personal interest. In this case, designating the property with the greatest interest expense as a second home will likely make the most sense. Another option is to open up one of the properties to rental use. This could allow you to deduct the mortgage interest from all three properties: your primary residence, the second home, and the rental property. For detailed information on deducting qualified mortgage interest on a second home and its limits, read Chapter 2.

Exclusive Rental Use

At the other end of the spectrum is a property used exclusively as a rental. In this case, you must report all rental income, but you can also report all rental expenses. And you may be able to deduct rental expenses even if they are more than the gross rental income. The details of available expenses and deductions for a property used exclusively as a rental are discussed in Chapters 2 and 3.

Mixed Personal Use and Rental Use

In reality, most vacation home owners use their property for both personal and rental use. The tax treatment that applies to mixed-use vacation properties hinges on how often the property is rented. If you rent a vacation property that you also use for personal time, then you need to understand the following rules and strategies.

Nominal Rental Use

First, if you rent out your vacation home for fourteen days or less during the year, none of the income is taxable! This can be a nice little loophole for those with vacation properties in high demand during a certain time of year. For example, the owner of a condominium in Vail Village who uses the property primarily for personal use may be able to rent her property for two weeks around Christmas (prime ski season) and make $500/night for a total of $7,000 tax free. The flip side is that you are not permitted to report any rental expenses if you rent your property for fourteen days or less during the year.

Property Used as a Home

If you rent your vacation home for more than fourteen days during the year, then you must report and pay taxes on the rental income, and you must divide your expenses between rental use and personal use because only the rental expenses are deductable. This is true regardless of how much you use your property for personal use, even if it is only one day.

However, the extent to which rental expenses can be deducted depends on whether the vacation property is considered a dwelling unit used as a home. If it is, you cannot report rental expenses that are more than your gross rental income, although losses can be carried forward and used in later years to offset future rental income.

The IRS considers most properties as dwelling units with the exception of hotel or motel rooms. A dwelling unit is simply a property with basic living accommodations, such as sleeping space, a toilet, and cooking facilities. It may be a house, apartment, condominium, mobile home, boat, or vacation home.

The more important question is whether you use your dwelling unit as a home. You use a dwelling unit as a home if during the year you use it for personal purposes for more than the greater of:

➤ Fourteen days, or
➤ 10 percent of the total days it is rented to others at a fair rental price.

For example, assume you rent your vacation home for 150 days at market rates during the year and you use the home for personal use for sixteen days. Your sixteen days of personal use exceeds 10 percent of 150 days, which is fifteen days (which is greater than fourteen days). In this case, the IRS will treat you as having used the property as a home that year.

So what is a personal use day? A day of personal use is any day that the property is used by any of the following people.

1. You or any other person who has an interest in it, unless you rent it to another owner as her primary house under a shared equity financing agreement (which we will explain later).
2. A member of your family or a member of the family of any other person who has an interest in it, unless the family member uses the property as her main home and pays a fair rental price. Family includes brothers, sisters, half brothers and half sisters, spouses, ancestors (like parents and grandparents), and lineal descendants (like children and grandchildren).
3. Anyone under an arrangement that lets you use some other property.
4. Anyone at less than fair rental price.

There are a few phrases here that warrant explanation. First, many people have not heard of a shared equity financing agreement, or SEFA. Generally speaking, this is an agreement where two or more people buy a property (including the land) and one or more of the co-owners is entitled to occupy the property as his main home upon payment of fair rent to the other co-owner or owners.

Second, what is a fair rental price? Generally, the fair rental price is equal to the price charged in the area for similar properties. As you might guess, the steeply discounted rate you charge a family member for using your beach cottage for a weekend is not a fair rental price and, therefore, would constitute personal use days by you.

There are several important exceptions to what is considered a personal use day. These exceptions can be very useful in borderline situations. When counting days of personal use, the following days are excluded.

SHARED EQUITY FINANCING AGREEMENT

SEFAs can be used by a parent to help an adult child purchase a home by combining each party's resources to pay the down payment and closing costs. Instead of making a loan to the child, the parent takes an equity interest in the property and qualifies for rental property tax benefits. Essentially the parent becomes an investor/owner, and the child becomes the occupant/owner.

1. Days spent substantially repairing or maintaining the property even if your family uses it for recreational purposes on the same day.
2. Days you used the property as your main home before or after renting it or offering it for rent if you rented or tried to rent the property for more than twelve consecutive months, or you rented or tried to rent it for less than twelve consecutive months and the period ended because you sold or exchanged the property.
3. Days spent in the property by a co-owner who uses it as his main home under a shared equity financing agreement.

The most commonly used exception is for repair and maintenance. For example, the three days you spend each September repairing any damage caused by renters would not be counted as personal use days.

The point of counting all of these days is to determine your rental expense deductions. If you have used the property as a home during the year, then the amount of rental expenses that may be deducted cannot exceed the rental income from the property.

Nominal Personal Use

If you do not use the property as a home, then you are allowed to fully deduct the rental expenses, subject to the loss limits we covered in Chapter 3. Keep in mind that in most cases, rental income from a vacation home will be passive. Net losses from the vacation rental are passive unless the taxpayer materially participates. Materially participating is often unlikely since many vacation rentals have a management company and are located far away from the taxpayer's residence. Chapter 3 discusses the material participation requirement in more detail.

Dividing Expenses

If you need to divide expenses between rental and personal purposes, the breakout is based on the number of days used for each purpose. When dividing your expenses, follow these rules.

➤ Any day that the property is rented at a fair rental price is considered a rental day even if you used the property for personal purposes that day. This rule does not apply when determining if you used the property as a home.

➤ Any day that the property is available for rent but not actually rented is not a day of rental use.

Many vacation homes are owned by more than one person. If this is the case, you will need to further divide the rental-use expenses based on each owner's interest in the property. Many vacation properties today are owned by multiple investors through organized fractional or time-share programs. This type of multiowner structure presents unique issues that we outline below.

TIME-SHARES

Time-shares have become a very popular method of owning a vacation property. More people can afford a one-twelfth interest in a $500,000 vacation condominium than can afford the entire condominium. Plus, the offerings are numerous and varied, so there is something for everyone. Enter any resort town and you can easily wind up touring a time-share property or watching a marketing film. Like us, maybe you have done this after being offered a free dinner or some other goodie.

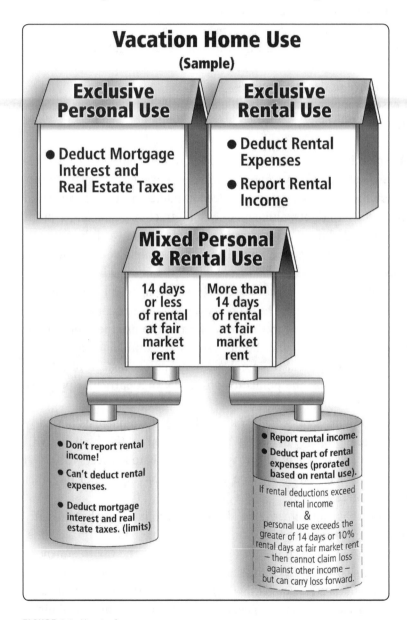

FIGURE 4.1 Vacation home use

As with other forms of vacation property ownership, time-shares have tax implications. The tax treatment of time-share vacation properties, just like wholly owned vacation properties, is tied to the extent to which the property is used for personal or rental use.

There are basically three ways time-shares are structured:

➤ Fee simple or deeded interests
➤ Lease arrangements or right-to-use interests
➤ The point system

As you might guess, fee simple or deeded fractional time-share ownership is most similar to what we normally consider property ownership since the purchaser receives a deeded interest in the property and related ownership rights, although only for a fraction of the entire property. Most deeded time-share interests are sold in one-week increments. In the United States, deeded time-share interests are a common form of time-shares.

In contrast, under a right-to-use or lease arrangement the developer ultimately holds the title to the property. The purchaser obtains an interest in the property that is in the form of a right to use the property for a designated period of time. Point systems are similar to right-to-use arrangements except that the purchaser buys points instead of a lease, and the ability to use the points toward a stay in a particular property expires on a set date.

Since fee simple or deeded fractional time-share interests normally represent a real property interest, which is the focus of this book, we will focus on the tax treatment of this type of time-share interest. Talk with your tax advisor if you own or are considering buying one of the other time-share interests.

The purchase agreement of a deeded fractional time-share usually spells out the usage rules based on one of four methods: (1) fixed time, (2) floating time, (3) open use, or (4) point system. The tax treatment of deeded time-share interests is the same regardless of the usage rules. Most deeded time-share arrangements will be governed just like the other vacation properties discussed in this chapter, and the tax treatment will hinge on the extent to which the property is used for personal or rental use.

Only qualifying mortgage interest and property taxes are deductible if the property is used exclusively for personal use. Remember from Chapter 2 that to be considered a qualified residence interest the time-share must be a second residence, and total indebtedness for both the primary and secondary residences must not exceed $1 million.

The type and use of the loan may impact the availability of the mortgage interest deduction. Interest paid or accrued on a home equity loan used to purchase a time-share interest may be treated as qualified residence interest, provided the loan does not exceed $100,000. However, if a consumer loan instead of a mortgage is used to obtain the time-share, none of the interest expense is deductible. This is an important point to keep in mind since financing for time-share interests is not as readily available as it is for home purchases and may take alternative forms. Oftentimes, the developer of a time-share property will also be the lender.

While more tax benefits and deductions are available if the time-share property is used for rental purposes, be aware that the IRS combines the use of all owners of a given time-share unit when counting days of personal and rental use. Accordingly, it is unlikely that a time-share owner will qualify for tax-free rental income treatment since the IRS counts the number of rental days for the entire unit when determining compliance with the fourteen-day or less rental requirement, not just a given time-share owner's portion.

The result is that, in most cases, time-share rental income will be taxed and you will need to allocate expenses between personal and rental use. It is also unlikely that you will be able to deduct a loss that exceeds the gross rental income, since the IRS considers the use of every person owning an interest in the time-share unit when counting days of use for the fourteen-day/10 percent cap on personal use.

SELLING YOUR VACATION HOME

Selling your vacation home is generally no different than selling any other real estate investment property. In most cases, gain from the sale will be taxed at the capital gain rate. If you have owned the property for more than a year, the preferential 15 percent long-term capital gain rate could apply. And by using the property as a rental you could qualify for a like-kind exchange or installment sale.

In addition, you may be able to move into the property and qualify for the principal residence exclusion of $250,000/person and $500,000/couple. Proceed with caution here. Generally, as long as the owner has used the property as a primary residence for two years then the principal residence exclusion is available. However, the owner cannot claim the $250,000/$500,000 exclusion if she acquired the property in a like-kind exchange within the last five years. There are also other limitations and requirements for claiming the primary residence exclusion that are discussed in Chapter 5.

Also beware that any depreciation taken on the property when it was an investment will still be recaptured and taxed on a subsequent sale of a property converted to a primary residence, even if the principal residence exclusion is available.

CLOSING NOTES

A vacation home can be a great way to combine a tax-advantaged investment with a vacation retreat. As popular as vacation homes are becoming, you would think the tax rules would have been simplified, but they are fairly complex. Your tax strategies will depend on how you use the property, and you will need to carefully count and track days of personal use and rental use. A few final notes to close this chapter are listed below.

➤ If you rent a vacation home for fourteen days or less in a year, the income is tax free but you cannot deduct any rental expenses. If you rent a vacation home for more than fourteen days, you must divide your expenses between rental use and personal use.

➤ If you use your vacation home during the year for personal use more than the greater of fourteen days or 10 percent of the total days it is rented to others at a fair rental price, then it will be considered a home. You must prorate your deductions based on how many days the property was rented at a fair rental price during the year. Also, your losses cannot offset more than the gross rental income from the property. You can, however, carry the losses forward as suspended losses to use in later years.

➤ If you used the property for personal use but did not use it enough to be considered a home, you still must divide the expenses between personal use and rental use, but you can potentially offset income from other sources with losses from the property in excess of gross rental income, subject to the at-risk rules and passive activity loss rules we cover in Chapter 3.

➤ Personal-use days do not include days substantially spent maintaining and repairing your vacation property—even if your kids are with you.

➤ Deeded fractional interest time-shares are subject to the same rules as other vacation properties, but it is highly unlikely you could claim tax-free income based on the fourteen days or less rental rule. This is because the IRS counts the number of rental days for the entire property, not just one owner.

➤ It is possible to convert your vacation home into a primary residence and qualify for the $250,000/$500,000 primary residence exclusion; however, such a conversion can take up to five years and is subject to several other requirements.

PART TWO
Sell Real Estate Without Paying Taxes

CHAPTER 5

Home Sweet (Tax-Free) Home

Owning your own home is America's unique recipe for
avoiding revolution and promoting pseudo-equality at the
same time.

—Florence King, American writer and conservative columnist

Owning a home is clearly part of the American Dream. The National Association of Realtors projects that the homeownership rate in the United States could exceed 70 percent by the year 2013. A home provides shelter and security, and it can also generate significant wealth. A large part of the wealth created by homes is due to the generous tax incentives provided to home owners in the Internal Revenue Code. For example, while most consumer interest is not deductable, residential mortgage interest is largely deductable. The greatest potential benefit to homeowners comes in the exclusion of gains from the sale of a principal residence. In this chapter, we cover the specific tax rules regarding treatment of gain or loss from the sale of a primary residence.

THE PRINCIPAL RESIDENCE EXCLUSION

The principal residence exclusion, in IRC Section 121, allows an individual to exclude from income up to $250,000 of gain on the sale of a principal residence. In most cases, married couples filing a joint return can exclude up to $500,000 of gain from income. The exclusion can be used by taxpayers of any age and as often as every two years (and in some cases more frequently).

The current rules are found in the Taxpayer Relief Act of 1997, which simplified and expanded the rules applied to the sale of a primary residence. Prior to the 1997 Act, the rules were most beneficial to homeowners aged fifty-five and over (the age fifty-five exemption) and those who purchased a new home of greater value (the rollover rule). The rollover rule was eliminated entirely for sales and exchanges after May 6, 1997. The result of the changes is that the exclusion now applies to homeowners of any age and does not penalize those who downsize or move to a lower-value home.

Another simplification of the 1997 Act was to reduce filing requirements. You do not need to report the sale of your home on your tax return if you can exclude all of the gain. If there is any taxable gain above the dollar limitation of $250,000 for an individual or $500,000 for a married couple, the entire gain and the amount of the prorated exclusion is reported.

While this is one of the simplest rules in the tax code, there are a couple of requirements that can trip up taxpayers. First, the exclusion is for gain from the sale of a principal residence, not an investment property. So you must be able to prove that the property that was sold is your principal residence (known as the ownership and use test). Most of us think of our principal residence as the home that we live in for a majority of each year, and most of the time that is the case.

Second, to be a completely tax-free sale, the gain must be equal to or less than the $250,000/$500,000 maximum allowable exclusion. The dollar limit is set high enough that most people do not exceed it; however, if you live in a high-value home or in a rapidly appreciating community, or both, you need to plan carefully to manage any gain that is outside the maximum allowable exclusion. The sections that follow analyze the ownership and use tests and how to calculate gain or loss for the maximum allowable exclusion in more detail.

Ownership and Use Tests

The ownership and use tests require that during the five-year period that ends on the date of the sale, you must have owned and used the property as a principal residence for periods aggregating two years or more. The two-year period is counted as 730 (365 x 2) days or twenty-four full months.

Because the two-year period use requirement is aggregated over five years and does not need to be concurrent, there is some flexibility to the rule. Short, temporary absences are counted as periods of use even if the home is rented out during the absence. An absence due to time spent in a nursing home for physical or mental incapacity will not count against the two-year period as long as the individual owned and used the property as a principal residence for a total of one year during the five years preceding a sale or exchange.

Counting days is as important to the principal residence tax rules as it is to the rules applied to vacation properties in Chapter 4. When you own a principal residence and a vacation property you need to carefully count, allocate, and record days of use in order to maximize the tax benefits applied to each of the properties.

> *Example:* The Kendalls, like many baby boomers, have a second home that they use for extended vacations. Their primary home is in Colorado Springs. They spend two months out of each year at their vacation home in Aspen. They will not jeopardize their Colorado Springs home being a principal residence as long as both tests are met during the five-year period that ends on the date of sale.

In order for married individuals filing a joint return to qualify for the $500,000 exclusion, both spouses must meet the two-year use test and neither spouse must have used the principal residence exclusion for any other sale or exchange during the previous two years. While each spouse must meet the use test, only one spouse needs to fulfill the ownership test. This means that title to the principal residence can be in the name of only one spouse.

Newly Married

The most confusion arises in the case of newly married couples where one or both spouses own a home before the marriage. When only one spouse owns a home prior to the marriage, the couple will probably need to live in that home for two years to qualify for the combined $500,000 exclusion. Otherwise, if they sell the home soon after getting married, they will be limited to the $250,000 exclusion on an individual basis.

In cases where each person owns a home before marriage, it is possible for the couple to seek the $500,000 exclusion on both homes. Doing so would require establishing joint use of each home for the requisite two-year period. In other words, live in one home for two years, sell it, and then move into the other home for two years before selling it. This method is a bit like playing musical houses, but it may be worth the effort given the possibility of exempting $500,000 of gain on each home (for a total of $1 million) from a 15 percent federal capital gain rate (plus any state income or capital gains taxes).

Impact of Death or Divorce

Death and divorce can impact the ownership and use test. When a spouse dies before the date of sale, the surviving spouse is considered as owning and living in the home for the same period as the deceased spouse as long as the surviving spouse has not remarried before the date of sale. If the surviving spouse remarries before the date of sale, then the newly married couple will have to start counting anew in order to qualify for the combined exclusion.

In cases where a residence is transferred to an individual incident to a divorce, the time during which the individual's former spouse owned the residence is added to the individual's period of ownership. In addition, an individual is treated as using property as a principal residence for any period of ownership while the individual's former spouse is granted use of the property under a divorce or separation instrument. This means that if the nonresiding spouse and the former spouse jointly own the home and agree to sell it only after the children have been emancipated, the nonresiding spouse may still qualify for the exclusion.

Residence Acquired Through Like-Kind Exchange

There is a special rule for principal residences previously acquired in a Section 1031 like-kind exchange. If you acquire a property through a like-kind exchange and decide to live in it as a principal residence, you will need to hold the property for five years before Section 121 can be used to exclude gain from a sale. The five-year holding period begins on the date of acquisition of the property. Chapter 7 covers Section 1031 exchanges in more detail.

Example: Rob decides to sell a commercial building he owns. To avoid recognizing taxable gain on a sale, he exchanges the building for a condominium in a 1031 tax-deferred transaction. He acquires the replacement condominium on January 1, 2002 as an investment property and rents it through January 1, 2003. He begins using the condominium as a personal residence on January 2, 2003 and sells the property on January 15, 2005. Despite satisfying the two-year ownership and use tests, Rob will recognize all gain on the sale of the condominium since he did not hold the replacement property for five years.

Special Circumstances

There may be cases where an individual was on track to meet the ownership and use tests but was prohibited due to events beyond her control. The IRS tries to accommodate these special circumstances. In some cases, the two-year ownership and use test period may be suspended, and in others it may be waived and the dollar limit for the exclusion reduced.

Military Service

There is a special exception to the two-out-of-five-year rule for military and Foreign Service personnel who are called to active duty away from home. Those serving on qualified official extended duty as a member of the uniformed services or of the Foreign Service of the United States can choose to suspend the running of the five-year period for up to ten years. The election is effective during the time within which the individual or his or her spouse is on qualified official extended duty, meaning serving at a duty station or residing in government quarters under government orders at least fifty miles from the principal residence for a period greater than ninety days or for an indefinite time.

Employment, Health, and Other

Any individual who fails to meet the ownership and use tests may be eligible for a partial exclusion if his primary reason for selling the home is due to one of the following:

➤ A change in place of employment;
➤ Health reasons; or
➤ Unforeseen circumstances.

The IRS will consider all of the facts and circumstances related to the reason for sale, including the individual's financial ability to maintain the property and material changes that make it impracticable to remain in the home. The primary reason for the sale will automatically be treated as having been due to employment, health, or unforeseen circumstances if one of the safe harbor tests is met.

The safe harbor test for change in place of employment is met if the individual's new place of employment is located at least fifty miles farther from the home sold than the former place of employment. The safe harbor test for health reasons is met if moving is necessary to obtain, provide, or facilitate the diagnosis, cure, mitigation, or treatment of disease, illness, or injury for one's self or a qualified individual such as a spouse or family member. Examples of unforeseen circumstances that have been recognized by the IRS include:

➤ Condemnation, seizure, or other involuntary conversion of the home;
➤ Damage to the home from natural or manmade disasters or acts of terrorism;
➤ Death;
➤ Change in employment status that qualifies the individual for unemployment benefits or that makes it impossible to pay a mortgage or reasonable basic living expenses;
➤ Divorce or legal separation; and
➤ Multiple births from a single pregnancy.

The reduced exclusion under these special circumstances is a prorata amount of the maximum allowable exclusion ($250,000 or $500,000) based on the actual period of ownership or use during the five-year period ending on the sale date, or the period between the most recent prior sale and the current sale divided by twenty-four months or 730 days. Essentially, the partial exclusion is based on how long you were in the home.

Calculating Gain or Loss

While selling a home can be emotionally taxing, it is rarely financially taxing. Most of the time homes are sold for a gain that is completely tax free! However, if you live in a high-value home or in a rapidly appreciating community, or both, you need to plan carefully to manage any gain that is outside the maximum allowable exclusion.

When calculating gain or loss on the sale of a home, you need to first determine the following amounts.

➤ Selling price
➤ Selling expenses
➤ Amount realized (selling price minus selling expenses)
➤ Adjusted basis

The selling price is the easiest amount to figure out; it is the total amount of sales proceeds received for the home. In most cases, this amount will consist of cash received, but it could include notes, debts assumed by the buyer, and the fair market value of any services or property received by the seller. Selling expenses include broker commissions, title and closing costs, and other closing-related expenses. The selling price is subtracted from the selling expenses to determine the amount realized.

Recall from Chapter 1 that basis or cost basis is a financial term that refers generally to the amount of one's investment in a property for tax purposes. A property's cost basis is usually equal to the purchase price of the property plus certain settlement fees. The basis may be adjusted up or down over time for several factors that result in the adjusted basis.

Once these amounts are determined, they can be plugged into the following equation to determine whether you have made money or lost money on the sale of your home.

Capital Gain (or Loss) = Amount Realized – Adjusted Basis

To compute your taxable gain, simply subtract any capital gain from the applicable maximum allowable exclusion (either $250,000 or $500,000). Figure 5.1 shows an example of how this calculation works.

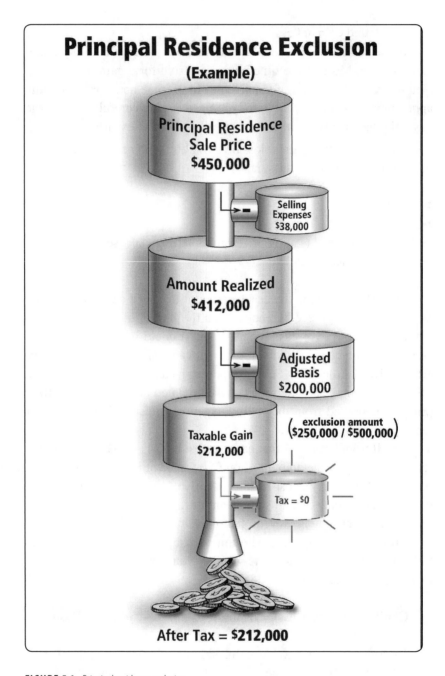

FIGURE 5.1 Principal residence exclusion

Impact of Business Use and Rental Income

Many people use their home for business or to produce rental income, and it is possible to take advantage of the principal residence exclusion in these cases. Allowing the principal residence exclusion to be used for residences that contain home offices is especially important today since large numbers of people telecommute or work from home. The key to the tax treatment in this scenario is still whether you satisfy the ownership and use tests.

Example: Rachel bought a house in 2000 and lived in it for one year. In 2001, she moved out and rented the house for eighteen months. Once the renter's lease expired, she decided to move back in and live in the home until selling it in 2005. Rachel may exclude up to $250,000 of gain from the sale since she lived in the home for a total of more than two years during the five-year period preceding the sale. However, Rachel cannot exclude the part of the gain attributable to any depreciation she claimed or could have claimed for renting the house.

You will be required to pay tax on gain from the sale of a principal residence to the extent of any depreciation allowable with respect to business or rental use after May 6, 1997. This is referred to as recapturing depreciation. The pros and cons of taking deductions for business use of your home are discussed in Chapter 2.

If you use the property partly as a home and partly as a business or rental, the tax treatment depends on whether the business or rental is in the same dwelling unit as your home or is in a separate building or apartment. If the business or rental is in the same dwelling unit as your principal residence, then you may claim the exclusion for the entire property.

Example: Steve sold his home in 2007 and made $50,000 of gain on the sale. In the year before the sale he claimed $750 of depreciation for part of the home that he used as a business office. This business office was in the basement of his home. Steve should report $50,000 of realized gain, $50,000 of excluded gain for the Section 121 or principal residence exclusion, and $750 of depreciation recapture.

If the business or rental is in a separate dwelling unit, like an apartment, then you must treat the sale as a sale of two properties: one principal residence and one business or rental property. The basis in the entire property and any gain is divided between the home and business portions of the property, and they are treated separately for tax purposes. The principal residence exclusion applies only to the part of the property used as a home, and the part of the property used for business or rental is treated as a sale of business property to which different tax rules apply.

The tax regulations give several other examples that the IRS considers a separate part of the property used for business or rental income:

➤ A working farm on which your house is located;
➤ An apartment building in which you live in one unit and rent the others; or
➤ A store building with an upstairs apartment in which you lived.

Remember, you cannot exclude gain on the separate part of your property used for business or to produce rental income unless you owned and lived in that part of your property as your main home for at least two years during the five-year period ending on the date of the sale. Even when the use test is met for the separate business part, if there was business use in the year of sale, you must treat the sale as a sale of two properties and report each separately. The maximum allowable exclusion will be divided between the part of the property used for business and the part used as a separate home. Allowing use to be fractionally divided like this is helpful to those who own and live in an apartment building or multiunit property.

If there was no business use in the year of sale and the use test for both the business or rental part and the part you use as a home has been met, you do not need to treat the transaction as the sale of two properties.

Involuntary Conversion

What happens if the principal residence is destroyed, stolen, seized, requisitioned, condemned, or sold under a threat of condemnation (known as an involuntary conversion)? In most of these cases, the individual whose property was converted will receive some compensation for the property. For example, if the government takes a person's home to make way for a new road, the person will receive a condemnation award to cover the loss of the property. Another example is receiving insurance proceeds for the loss of a home due to fire or hurricane damage.

An involuntary conversion of a residence is treated as a sale or exchange for purposes of the Section 121 exclusion discussed in this chapter. If your principal residence is involuntarily converted, then you may treat the home as having been sold and exclude the gain up to the $250,000 or $500,000 limit, whichever applies. If the total realized gain is more than the applicable dollar limit for the principal residence exclusion, then recognition of the excess may be deferred if a replacement property is purchased within the specified replacement period.

Loss on a Principal Residence

Unfortunately, there is not much to say if you have a loss on the sale of a principal residence. A loss on the sale of a principal residence is treated as a personal expense and cannot be deducted from income. Hopefully, you can wait to sell your home when the market shifts upward again.

If you are in the unfortunate position of having to take a loss on the sale of a principal residence, one option may be to convert your devalued home into a business or investment property so that you can deduct the loss when you sell. Of course, you would need to carefully review the rules regarding business and investment properties to make sure the change in characterization is legitimate under the tax code. Expenses and losses attributable to investment properties are discussed in more detail in Chapters 2 and 3.

The best choice when faced with a loss may be to hold on to the property. If you need cash, you could rent all or part of the property. Of course, if you rent the entire property you will need to find a new home for yourself. Another option for individuals age sixty-two years or older is to use a reverse mortgage to convert some of the equity into cash without having to sell the home. A reverse mortgage does not need to be repaid until the borrower dies, sells the home, or moves permanently out of the home. For more information on reverse mortgages, see *The Complete Guide to Reverse Mortgages* (Adams Media).

MAXIMIZING THE BENEFITS

In this section we outline strategies and tips to maximize your use of the principal residence exclusion. Keep in mind, however, that these strategies and tips are concerned primarily with maximizing your bottom line. Some of these strategies can be very disruptive to your lifestyle, and many taxpayers prefer simply to use the primary residence exclusion if and when they move. In addition, some of these strategies can get tricky, so always talk with your tax advisor.

Fix, Wait, and Flip

For those who do not mind moving to a new home every two years, one way to build wealth is to repeatedly purchase property, fix it up, live in it for two years, and then sell it utilizing the principal residence exclusion. This strategy may require a good cash reserve for remodeling expenses, unless you are a handyman and have extra time. It also requires good judgment about which properties will see significant appreciation during the two-year holding period. Still, this can be a great way to work up to a higher-value home, and it can get you into the higher-value home much faster than saving paychecks.

> *Example:* Julie and Eric got married and bought their first home for $119,000. The home was small, but it was located in a well-established and desirable neighborhood. They painted the interior, remodeled a bathroom, and sold the home two and a half years later for $151,000. The gain was completely tax free and they used it to purchase another home for $289,500. Julie and Eric lived in this home and fixed it up over a period of four years. This home sold for $365,000, and they purchased their dream home for $525,000. In just six years, they were able to purchase their dream home. It would have taken them twice as long or more to save money from regular income to make a down payment on such a home.

Managing Excess Gain

While the maximum allowable exclusion seems high, it is possible for taxpayers selling their homes to end up with a gain in excess of the exclusion. Owners of high-value homes come to mind, but so do homeowners in rapidly appreciating real estate markets. Think back a couple of years to Phoenix, Las Vegas, and parts of Florida and California. Hot real estate markets have been known to appreciate as much as 40 percent in just a few years. Even above-average appreciation over time can provide substantial gain. Those who purchased homes decades ago did so at a small fraction of what they are worth today. In the next sections, we discuss ways to manage excess gain through the use of capital improvements, capital losses, and different types of sales.

Capital Improvements

One possible way to offset high appreciation is to increase the adjusted basis through capital improvements. An average bathroom remodel can cost $15,000, and the cost of an average kitchen remodel can be as high as $50,000 to $80,000. Such improvements could, however, create even more gain by increasing the value of the property more than the cost of the improvement. So this approach may not work in many situations.

Separating Extra Acreage

If your home includes surrounding lots or acreage that will result in taxable gain over the maximum allowable exclusion, it may be best to not include the additional acreage as part of the principal residence. Instead, you might be able to claim the extra acreage is eligible for a like-kind exchange due to an investment or business use. Separating acreage like this requires careful analysis since business use of a portion of a principal residence is inconsistent with the Section 121 exclusion.

Capital Losses

If it is obvious that when you sell your home it will be at a gain that will exceed the maximum allowable exclusion, then you may want to coordinate the sale with capital loss recognition. The year that your capital losses are running high may be a good year to sell your home. Or if you must sell your home in a given year, maybe that year is a good time to sell any assets that will create a capital loss.

Sales to Related Parties

The principal residence exclusion does not apply to a sale of a remainder interest in the home where the person acquiring the home is a member of the taxpayer's family or other related entity. The sale of remainder interest might be a sale subject to the right of the seller to live in the property until death. Outside of remainder interest transactions, there may be some relief available through selling to a related party or entity. Of course, transactions that lack substance are always subject to IRS scrutiny. And there may be gift-tax consequences if the home is sold for a bargain price.

Installment Sales

An installment sale is a transaction in which the sales price is paid through a series of payments known as installments. The receipt of the full sales price is spread over a period of time, and so is the payment of taxes on the gain. Installment sales and the reporting requirements for them are governed by IRC Section 453 and are discussed in more detail in Chapter 6. For taxpayers whose top dollars are taxed at 25 percent or more and where taxable long-term capital gain is substantial, selling a principal residence in conjunction with an installment sale can reduce or eliminate the effect of various phaseouts of tax deductions and reduce the exposure of ordinary income to the alternative minimum tax.

Leave It to the Heirs

Another option for older homeowners is to not sell the home when it is likely to create a large taxable gain. Continue holding the property and leave it to your heirs. If the property is likely to pass to the homeowner's heirs before 2010, the basis in the property will be stepped up to its date-of-death value, and any appreciation in value during the decedent's life would escape tax.

Convert to an Investment Property

It is possible to convert your principal residence into an investment property by renting it and then using a like-kind exchange to completely defer your taxable gain. However, in most cases this strategy is not preferred because a like-kind exchange only defers taxes, while the principal residence exclusion eliminates taxes. That is why the more common desire for a taxpayer is to convert an investment property into a principal residence in order to take advantage of the $250,000/$500,000 exclusion.

This conversion can be tricky. If you purchased an investment property in a like-kind exchange, you must use it as an investment property for some time after the exchange. If you immediately move into the property you will disqualify the exchange. You must also be able to show your intent in acquiring the replacement property was for investment (or for trade or business) purposes. For this reason, documenting your investment reasons and related investigations prior to exchanging any property is a good idea. That way you will be able to prove your intended use of the acquired property was investment (or trade or business) even if you later used it as your main home.

Finally, as discussed above, if you acquired a property in a like-kind exchange you cannot claim the principal residence exclusion for five years, regardless of whether you meet the standard two-year ownership and use rules before that time.

CLOSING NOTES

The first purchase of just about any real estate investor should be a home. The tax code practically begs taxpayers to buy a home. As you know from this chapter and Chapter 2, which covered residential mortgage interest deductions and property tax deductions, the tax code provides generous tax incentives to owners of principal residences. In fact, home appreciation coupled with these tax benefits have created more net worth for more Americans than probably any other tax rule. On the next page are a few final notes to close this chapter.

➤ You may exclude up to $250,000 of gain, or $500,000 for married couples filing a joint return, from the sale of a principal residence.

➤ To qualify you must have owned the property and used it as a principal residence for two years out of the five years preceding the sale and not used the exclusion for any other property within two years prior to the sale.

➤ There is no limit to the number of times you can use this exclusion throughout your lifetime.

➤ If you acquired a property in a like-kind exchange, you cannot use the principal residence exclusion for at least five years.

➤ Even if you fail to meet the ownership and use tests, you may be eligible for a partial exclusion if the primary reason for selling your home was due to qualifying employment, health, or certain other unforeseen circumstances.

➤ You will not be able to use the principal residence exclusion for the part of your residence used for a business or to produce rental income.

CHAPTER 6

Defer Taxes with Installment Sales

Every man who invests in well-selected real estate in a growing section of a prosperous community adopts the surest method of becoming independent, for real estate is the basis of wealth.

—Theodore Roosevelt

Many successful investors would agree that real estate is the surest method for building wealth. They would also agree that buying well-selected real estate is the first step. But with real estate, it is the strategies available to defer taxation on profits on the disposition of property that can compound your returns and produce substantial wealth.

When you decide to dispose of a real estate investment, you basically have three options from a tax perspective:

1. Sell the property for cash and pay tax on the profit;
2. Sell the property in exchange for a loan from the buyer to create a future income stream; or
3. Exchange the property for other like-kind property.

There are certainly times when market conditions or personal circumstances dictate that selling the property and cashing out make the most sense, even with the tax bite. However, only options two and three can defer taxable gain and compound your return over time. So, if possible, you will want to choose option two or three. This chapter covers the second option, which is known as an installment sale, sometimes also referred to as seller financing or seller carry-back. We cover the third option, exchanging like-kind property, in Chapter 7.

INSTALLMENT SALE ESSENTIALS

The concept of an installment sale is pretty simple. The seller sells the property to the buyer, and, in lieu of a lump sum paid at closing, finances the buyer's purchase by agreeing to accept a series of scheduled payments in the future. For tax purposes, the IRS broadly defines an installment sale as "a disposition of property where at least one payment is to be received after the close of the taxable year in which the disposition occurs." There are a few exceptions to this broad definition, most notably when a dealer is involved, which we discuss later in this chapter. With an installment sale, gain must be reported under the installment method (pursuant to IRC Section 453) unless the taxpayer elects otherwise.

Why Installment Sales Make Sense

Why take on the risk of financing a buyer? One important reason is because installment sales can defer taxable profit and create a stream of income. Instead of paying tax on all of the profit in the year of the sale, the IRS allows you to report and pay taxes on only the pro-rata portion of your profit as you receive the cash. In addition to tax deferral, the ability to create a stream of income can be very helpful, especially with vacant land or property that does not generate rental income.

All Income Is Not Equal

Interest and rental income are taxed at ordinary income tax rates, which is almost always higher than the 15 percent long-term capital gain rate. However, income from installment sales is taxed at the lower long-term capital gain rate (to the extent it represents profit). A higher sales price and a lower interest rate can mean more profit taxed at the lower long-term capital gain rate.

A seller can also realize a higher rate of return through an installment sale note than if he had sold the property, paid the tax, and reinvested the proceeds. The higher rate of return comes from being able to earn interest on the taxable portion of the profit. This leverage can substantially enhance the seller's return compared with a similar after-tax investment return.

Plus, offering seller financing enhances the marketability of the real estate. Buyers usually react positively to the opportunity of having their purchase financed by the seller. In fact, this can justify a higher selling price. Seller financing almost always costs less and takes less time than bank financing. Most bank loans have a processing time of thirty to ninety days, and the costs typically include processing fees, appraisal fees, and discount points. In addition, sometimes seller financing may be the only realistic option available for a buyer. For example, banks typically will not make loans on more than 50 percent of the value of vacant land. So if a seller offers financing on vacant land, it can dramatically increase the marketability of the property.

How Installment Sales Work

Under the installment sales method, the taxpayer recognizes taxable gain only on the amount of gross profit received in the tax year. In most cases, payments received from an installment sale are only partially gross profit. How much of the payment is gross profit depends on what percentage of the total contract price from the deal is gross profit. This computation can be broken down into three steps.

1. Determine the total gross profit for the sale.
2. Determine the gross profit percentage for the sale.
3. For each taxable year, determine the taxable gain by multiplying the gross profit percent by the actual payments received.

The total gross profit on the sale is equal to the selling price minus the adjusted basis on the property sold. The gross profit percentage is equal to the ratio of the gross profit to the contract price.

> *Example:* Raj sold a small office building (adjusted basis of $200,000) to Tony for $500,000. He received $50,000 in cash at closing and the remaining balance was to be paid the following year with interest. Raj's gross profit is $300,000 ($500,000 – $200,000), and the gross profit percentage is 60 percent ($300,000 profit /$500,000 contract price). His taxable income for the year of the sale is $30,000 (60% x $50,000). The remaining $270,000 ($300,000 – $30,000) of gain will be taxable in the following year.

In our example, we assumed Raj did not have a mortgage. If Raj had a mortgage secured by the property that was paid off at closing, his total gross profit would include the excess, if any, of the amount the debt exceeded his adjusted basis. This excess would be taxable at the time of the sale even if he had not received enough cash at closing to pay the tax bill. If you have debt and are considering an installment sale, talk to your tax advisor first.

Installment Sales Payments

Each payment received on an installment sale has three components: (1) interest income, (2) return of adjusted basis, and (3) profit or gain on the sale. In our example, Raj's gross profit percentage was 60 percent, which means that 60 percent of each of his installment payments (excluding interest) is taxed at the capital gains tax rate. The remaining 40 percent of each installment payment (excluding interest) is a tax-free return of Raj's adjusted basis.

There is a big exception to the deferral of gain for depreciated property. Excess depreciation recapture (taxed at 25 percent) must be reported in full upon sale of the property, regardless of the amount of payments received. Avoid getting caught short by requiring enough cash at closing to pay your taxes. In fact, it may not make sense to use an installment sale with a property that is going to have significant depreciation recapture unless you get enough cash from the buyer at closing to cover the taxes.

Figure 6.1 shows the flow of cash for a sample installment sale.

The Interest Rate

Interest income, even on installment sales, is taxed at ordinary income tax rates. The amount of interest charged by the seller is called *stated interest*. Be aware that if the installment sale loan does not provide for adequate stated interest, the IRS will recharacterize part of the principal amount of the loan as interest. The IRS uses several tests to determine an adequate interest rate, including comparisons to the applicable federal rate. The applicable federal rates are prescribed rates published monthly by the IRS for certain loan terms. The rates can be found at *www.irs.gov* using the keywords "applicable federal rate." The IRS may attribute an interest payment to loans that charge interest below the applicable federal rate.

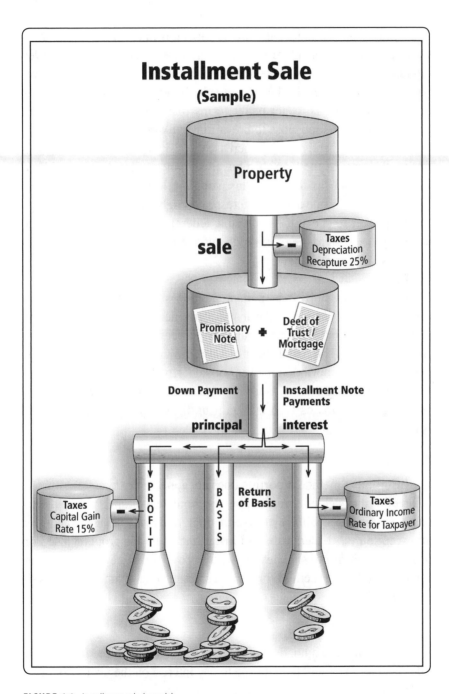

FIGURE 6.1 Installment sale (sample)

It may sound strange, but in many cases it is in the seller's best interest to charge a lower interest rate. Sellers often prefer to charge lower interest rates in order to make a reasonable purchase price increase and get more capital gains in the year of sale. In addition, one of the draws of seller financing is to get better terms than are available through a bank. A rate that is too close to prevailing bank rates may cause a buyer to look elsewhere and can also increase the risk of the buyer refinancing during the term of the loan. If a buyer refinances, your loan is paid off but you lose your tax deferral. Plus, you have lost your interest-bearing income stream. While a lower interest rate might avoid a premature payoff, remember to check the applicable federal rate and consult your tax advisor to make sure the rate is high enough to be adequate.

Electing Out

Installment reporting is mandatory for installment sales unless the taxpayer elects not to have the installment method apply. When might you elect to report the entire gain in the year of sale even though it is not required? The installment method only applies to realized gain. Losses must be reported in the year of sale. If you have suspended capital losses, then using the installment method could force you to delay your use of the losses to offset gain until later years when the gain is received.

Dealers

Installment method reporting does not apply to dealers. Recall from Chapter 1 that dealers are people who hold real property for sale to customers in the ordinary course of their trade or business. There is an exception for dealers using an installment sale for property used or produced in farming. And dealers who pay a special interest charge can use the installment method for certain sales of time-shares and residential lots.

Limits

Even if you are a nondealer, there are limitations to the installment sales benefits. You will be required to pay interest on the tax attributable to deferred installment gains to the extent that:

1. The selling price exceeds $150,000; and
2. The total installment obligations arising and outstanding at the close of any tax year exceed $5,000,000.

The interest is due on the part of the deferred gain in excess of $5,000,000. Tax liability is computed using the taxpayer's highest marginal tax rate for the current year. Interest is then charged on this tax liability using the applicable IRS underpayment rate.

Related Parties

The installment method is generally not available for reporting gain on the sale of depreciable real estate between related parties. Related parties include family members and corporations and partnerships that are owned more than 50 percent by the taxpayer. There are a few exceptions, including situations where it can be established that tax avoidance was not a motive of the sale. Nondepreciable property may be sold to a related party on an installment basis, but such a transaction is subject to scrutiny.

Key considerations that could disqualify the transaction include whether the parties intend to avoid taxes, whether the related purchaser disposes of the property before the seller receives all of the payments, and whether the related purchaser disposes of the property in a subsequent sale within two years of the first sale. A disqualified installment sale can result in the related seller being treated as having received the proceeds of the second disposition, thus accelerating the gain deferred on the original sale.

Escrow Accounts

The use of escrow accounts is another tricky area with installment sales. In general, seller-financed sales involving escrow accounts cannot be reported using the installment method. The IRS considers the buyer's obligation paid in full when the balance of the purchase price is deposited in the escrow account. The rationale is that the seller does not have to rely on the buyer for the payments; the seller relies on the escrow arrangement. It is possible to qualify an escrow arrangement for the installment method if it imposes substantial restrictions on the seller's right to receive the sale proceeds.

Combine Installment Sale with Like-Kind Exchange

In Chapter 7 we discuss like-kind exchanges, one of the most significant loopholes that exist for deferring taxable gain. Like-kind exchanges can be combined with installment sales under the right circumstances. By combining the two strategies you can step down to a smaller investment property and still defer taxable gains. You can also diversify your investments between real estate and holding a promissory note. If you receive an installment obligation in addition to like-kind property in an exchange, the following rules apply:

➤ The contract price is reduced by the fair market value of the like-kind property received in the exchange;
➤ The gross profit is reduced by any gain on the exchange that can be postponed; and
➤ Like-kind property received in the exchange is not considered payment on the installment obligation.

These rules shift more of the capital gain into the installment sale part of the transaction. There can be some really challenging issues that pop up when combining these two strategies, depending on whether the properties are mortgaged and the timing of the exchanges. Definitely consult your tax advisor before combining an installment sale and a like-kind exchange.

HOW TO STRUCTURE AN INSTALLMENT SALE

There are several risks associated with installment sales that can be lessened to some degree by properly structuring the installment sale. The major risks include default and foreclosure, early payoff, and lack of liquidity. In this section, we discuss these risks in connection with methods of balancing them. Some of these methods depend on negotiating the right financial terms, and others are legal or contractual protections.

Loan-to-Value Ratio

One of the first steps in seller financing is deciding on an acceptable loan-to-value ratio. A loan-to-value ratio is a measure of the amount of total financing in relation to the fair market value or sales price of a property. For example, an $800,000 loan on a $1,000,000 property has an 80 percent loan-to-value ratio. The rule is that the higher the loan-to-value ratio (lower down payment), the riskier the loan.

Lenders usually have a preferred loan-to-value ratio for different property types. An office building, for example, would probably have a lower preferred loan-to-value ratio than a townhome or a ten-unit apartment building. Ask a local bank representative or knowledgeable real estate agent for typical loan-to-value ratios for your particular property type and area. Keep in mind, however, that commercial lenders are very conservative and will not have as much information about your property as you do when deciding what type of security it provides.

In addition, part of your motivation in financing the sale is to achieve tax deferral benefits. A commercial lender does not have this added incentive. While a high down payment (lower loan-to-value ratio) provides more security, it will be taxed immediately as a payment received in the year of disposition. Depending on your comfort level with the buyer and the property, you may want to go with a lower than usual down payment. When assessing your comfort level with a buyer, ask yourself how long the buyer can afford to make regular payments and whether you trust the buyer to keep the property in good repair. If you are required to foreclose, which is costly and difficult, you want the property to be in a saleable condition when you take it back. Regardless of the buyer's position, the down payment should at least cover your selling expenses and any taxes due in the year of sale.

Term of Loan

Another important step in setting up a seller financing deal is to determine the term, or the length of time you are willing to carry the loan. Just like the loan-to-value ratio, you will need to consider your comfort level with the buyer and the type of property as well as your personal and financial circumstances. There are typically two numbers that you will hear: the amortization schedule and the actual term. Many institutional lenders amortize home loans over thirty years. If the loan payments are made on a monthly basis and include accumulated interest and some principal, it will take thirty years for the entire principal balance, including unpaid interest, to be paid in full.

Most sellers are not willing to finance a property for thirty years, so they create a shorter due date for the note, for example, five years. Of course, a buyer may not want the high monthly payments associated with a shorter term since it can significantly impact operating profits. A middle ground is to shorten the term but base the monthly payments on a longer amortization schedule, for example fifteen years, with a large balloon payment at the end of the term, such as five years, to make up the difference. This note would be referred to as a "fifteen due in five."

From a seller's perspective, a longer amortization schedule, like thirty years, results in the monthly payments consisting almost entirely of interest during the beginning years of the note. Through these large interest payments the seller is able to maximize the capital gains tax deferral and the interest earned on the deferred portion. Look at it this way, the large interest payments are cash in your pocket, and, if all goes as planned, you still get all of the principal back at the end of the term.

The term of the note is up to you, but as long as you are comfortable that the borrower will continue to pay on the note and that the property sufficiently secures the outstanding balance on the note, earning money on tax-deferred capital gains through an installment sale can beat most CDs by a long shot.

One final consideration when negotiating the loan-to-value ratio and the term of the loan is how these provisions will affect any resale of the note. Installment sale notes secured by real property are considered illiquid investments since there is no commonly and easily accessible resale market for these notes. A knowledgeable mortgage broker or Realtor in your area may be able to point you to someone willing to purchase your note, but beware. Because they are considered a high risk, buyers will expect a significant discount from the face value of the note. Even a strong note secured by a first-priority lien with a good loan-to-value ratio and an excellent borrower will be discounted. Second mortgages may face large discounts of up to fifty percent or more. Plus, if you sell your note, all your deferred gain will likely be recognized and the taxes will be owed. However, if the sale is at other than face value, gain or loss is recognized equal to the difference between the amount realized and your adjusted basis in the note on the date of the sale.

Prepayment Penalties

The flip side of wanting to sell your note is wanting to keep the income stream from the note for as long as possible. Presumably you chose to do this and are counting on the income for a number of years. A buyer who decides to pay off the note early can foil this goal. There is virtually no legal way to stop someone from paying off a loan early, so you cannot eliminate this risk. There are, however, legitimate ways to discourage early payoff.

The most common method is a prepayment penalty. There can be several legal restrictions on the amount of prepayment penalties that can be negotiated. Most of these protections apply only to residential property, not investment property. You will need to check the specific rules in your state before you determine a penalty. Aside from a penalty, the best way to discourage a borrower from early payoff is to set your terms and interest rates as favorably as possible while still protecting your security in the property and maximizing your return.

Even with a prepayment penalty, there are certain times when the buyer just needs to sell the property or pay off the note. For example, a borrower may need an equity line of credit or a second mortgage and be required to finance the entire property to avoid the equity line or second mortgage lender from having to take a second-priority lien against the property. The installment note holder may have the option of subordinating (that is, taking a back seat) to an equity line of credit or a home improvement loan, but this presents significant risks if the borrower is unable to pay on one or both notes.

Documenting an Installment Sale

Documenting an installment sale should involve a qualified attorney. Standard form agreements will usually not provide the necessary protections. Besides, as the lender you have the freedom to structure the deal to suit your circumstances, and you will want the documents tailored to accurately reflect the deal. The basic documents associated with seller financing include a promissory note and deed of trust (or mortgage) as a minimum and may include a security agreement, loan agreement, and UCC filing statement as well.

The general idea is that the promissory note reflects the legal obligation of the borrower to pay the lender/seller. The deed of trust (or mortgage) gives the lender a security interest in the property so that if the borrower does not comply with the terms and conditions of the promissory note, the lender has the right to force payment or foreclose and get the property back.

A loan agreement provides more substance than the simple promissory note. Pull out the loan documents from your home purchase and review the loan agreement. You may not want to use an agreement that dense, but many of the same provisions will apply when you are the lender in an installment sale. Any topics that are not addressed in the agreement lead to ambiguities that could cause a problem.

Think about what happens if the buyer decides to sell the property before the loan is repaid. A loan agreement with a prepayment penalty that complies with state law can provide some security for your income stream, but it may be best if the new buyer took over the loan obligations. A carefully drafted assumption clause allows the buyer to sell the property subject to assumable financing and gives you the ability to approve the new buyer's creditworthiness.

What if the buyer simply stops making loan payments? If it is a rental property, a provision for assignment of rents gives you the right to collect rents directly from tenants if your borrower defaults. A late fee and default interest clause substantially increases the rate of interest charge on amounts unpaid after their due date. If you do need to foreclose, you will want the property to be in good condition, and an inspection and maintenance provision will allow you to check up on the property. An insurance provision requires the borrower to maintain a minimum amount of property insurance and name you as a payee under the policy.

This is by no means a comprehensive list of loan provisions, but you get an idea of some of the more important provisions that may not be in a basic promissory note. Given the return on investment and tax savings at stake, it is worth spending some time and money to get properly drafted loan documents. You may be in the real estate investment business, not the lending business, but you will need to think like a lender when structuring your installment sale.

CLOSING NOTES ON INSTALLMENT SALES

Installment sales are a great way to defer taxable gain and create a stream of income. The ability to create a stream of income can be very helpful, especially with property that does not generate rental income, like vacant land, or in cases where an investor no longer wishes to manage a rental property. Installment sales have the added benefit of enabling an investor to earn interest on pretax dollars. That said, these transactions can be complicated and require careful structuring and drafting of the loan terms. A few more notes to close this chapter on installment sales are listed below.

➤ You must use installment method reporting whenever you receive at least one payment after the year of sale, unless you elect out of using the method.

➤ Under the installment method, all depreciation recapture is taxed at the time of the sale. Be sure to require enough cash at closing to cover this expense.

➤ Under the installment method, loan payments consist of interest income, tax-free return of capital, and taxable capital gain. Gain is only taxable when received. The amount of taxable gain in each payment is equal to a percentage of the total payment based on a ratio of gross profit to the contact price.

➤ You need to determine an adequate interest rate, loan-to-value ratio, and the term of the loan. In doing so, you need to weigh considerations such as maximizing deferral of capital gains, maximizing your return on investment, protecting your security interest in the property, and making the terms appealing to a buyer.

➤ In most cases, dealers cannot use the installment sales method. In addition, installment sales between family members or using escrow accounts usually do not work.

➤ You may want to elect out of the installment method if your mortgage exceeds your basis in the property or if you have suspended passive losses.

CHAPTER 7

Build Wealth with
Like-Kind Exchanges

A fellow can always get over losing money in a game of
chance but he seems so constituted that he can never get
over money thrown away to a government in taxes.

—Will Rogers

What if you could choose between paying your taxes now, paying them later, or not paying them at all? IRC Section 1031 gives real estate investors this choice. A 1031 exchange (or like-kind exchange) allows investors who exchange one property for another to defer the payment of taxes on gain that would otherwise be due on the sale of a property. The IRS treats such an exchange as a continuation of the original investment, not a sale, so that none of the gain is recognized for tax purposes. Remember from Chapter 1 that if gain is not recognized then no taxes are owed! There is no limit on the number of times you can complete a 1031 exchange, so it is possible to defer taxes indefinitely by continually exchanging properties.

In this chapter, we explain how a like-kind exchange works and provide tips and strategies for dealing with more complex exchanges. This is one of the longest chapters in the book, but it will be well worth your time. There is almost nothing else in the tax code that compares to the potential wealth multiplying affect of a like-kind exchange.

THE FOUNDATION OF LIKE-KIND EXCHANGES

The ability to defer taxable gain by exchanging one property (often called the *relinquished property*) for a new property (known as the *replacement property*) has been around in one form or another since about 1921. However, this tax-deferral strategy was rarely used in the early days because the IRS required the exchange to be simultaneous. In any real estate market, it would be unusual to find two property owners with similarly priced properties willing to swap them at the same time. Not surprisingly, investors who saw the wealth-building potential of a tax-deferred exchange began to challenge the simultaneous requirement.

A series of court decisions in the late 1970s and early 1980s, known collectively as the Starker cases, created the legal authority for a delayed exchange. A delayed exchange would allow an investor to close on the old property before finding and closing on the new property. The courts agreed with the IRS that if the property owner received funds from the sale, then the transaction looked more like a sale and subsequent purchase than an exchange. So it was decided that a third party would need to hold the proceeds from the sale, and the exchange would need to happen within a limited time period.

Today these transactions are known by many names, including 1031 exchanges, Starker exchanges, tax-deferred exchanges, like-kind exchanges (the name we typically use), and tax-free exchanges. No matter how it is referred to, many of our clients have created fortunes (and kept them!) by using like-kind exchange strategies.

THE NUTS AND BOLTS OF LIKE-KIND EXCHANGES

The key language of IRC Section 1031 says: "No gain or loss shall be recognized on the exchange of property held for productive use in a trade or business or for investment if such property is exchanged solely for property of like kind which is to be held either for productive use in a trade or business or for investment." As you can see in Figure 7.1, exchanging a property provides a very different tax result than selling a property.

FIGURE 7.1 Like-kind exchange

It sounds simple enough, but there are important details to understand. For example, what exactly is meant by "productive use in a trade or business or for investment"? What is property of a like kind? What if the exchanged properties are not the same value? The answers to many of the most common questions are provided in the following sections. Of course, every property and exchange is different, so if you have deal-specific questions, talk to your tax advisor.

There are six essential requirements that must be met for a transaction to qualify for a fully tax-deferred 1031 exchange.

1. The exchanged properties must be held for productive use in a trade or business or for investment.
2. The exchanged properties must be like-kind properties (properties of a similar nature or character).
3. The price of the replacement property must be equal to or greater than the price of the relinquished property.
4. The taxpayer cannot receive any proceeds or other assets (sometimes called "boot") from the transaction (this includes actual proceeds and proceeds deemed received through constructive receipt).
5. Qualified intermediaries must be used to facilitate the transaction.
6. The replacement property must be identified within the 45-day time limit and closed within the 180-day time limit.

In the sections that follow, we take a closer look at each of these requirements.

Property Used in a Trade or Business or Held for Investment
Whether a property is used in a trade or business or held for investment depends on how you use the property and characterize it on your tax returns. Both real and personal property can qualify for a like-kind exchange. We focus exclusively on real property; however, certain types of personal property also qualify for 1031 treatment, including boats, trucks, aircraft, and even cattle.

One of the easiest ways to identify an investment property is to understand what it is not. Clearly, property used primarily for personal use, such as a main home or a vacation property used primarily for personal use, is not an investment. Just because you hope your vacation home will appreciate in value does not make it an investment property where the primary purpose of the property is to be used for personal enjoyment.

In addition to property used primarily for personal purposes, property held primarily for sale does not qualify for like-kind exchange treatment. An example of property held primarily for sale is property a homebuilder builds primarily for sale to its customers. The tax code also excludes exchanges of stocks, bonds, or notes; other securities or indebtedness or interest; partnership interests; and certificates of trust or beneficial interests.

Real estate used in a taxpayer's trade or business and held for more than one year can qualify for a like-kind exchange. A typical example of a property that is used in a trade or business is a building owned for more than one year by a physician and used to operate his medical practice. While the building may qualify for 1031 treatment, any inventory or property that is held primarily for sale to customers will not qualify.

Like-Kind Property

As odd as the term "like-kind" sounds, it is one of the simplest requirements to meet. Like-kind simply means property of a similar nature or character (not quality or grade). The exchange of real estate for real estate or personal property for similar personal property is typically an exchange of like-kind property. So trading an apartment building for a vacant piece of ground is considered a like-kind exchange. This requirement gets more complicated with personal property, but almost any piece of real estate can be exchanged for another piece of real estate as long as both properties are held for productive use in a trade or business or for investment purposes.

How Do I Defer All Taxes on the Exchange?

If your goal is to defer all taxable gains on the exchange, you will need to be sure the replacement property has a purchase price that is equal to or greater than the selling price of the relinquished property. This rule can be satisfied in a number of ways. If there is a single relinquished property and multiple smaller replacement properties with a collective value equal to the relinquished property, then all taxable gain could be deferred.

WATCH OUT FOR FOREIGN PROPERTY.

There is an exception to this simple like-kind rule for foreign property. Real property located in the United States and real property located outside the United States are not considered like-kind property.

Or vice versa if multiple properties were sold and a single new replacement property was purchased for an equal or greater value, you still may be able to avoid taxable gain. For example, if you exchange an investment property valued at $100,000 for two replacement properties with an aggregate purchase price of $100,000, you could qualify for a completely tax-deferred like-kind exchange.

While most investors use like-kind exchanges to purchase properties of higher value (often referred to as "trading up"), it is possible to use an exchange even if the replacement property has a lower price than the relinquished property (this is called "trading down"). It just means that the difference is taxable.

> *Example:* Assume you purchased a property for $120,000 and it is now worth $250,000. You are now exchanging it for a replacement property worth $240,000. You would only recognize taxable gain of $10,000 (the difference between the value of your relinquished property and the value of the replacement property). If you had sold the property outright you would have had taxable gain of $130,000 (the difference between your sale price and your basis). Your potential tax savings could be $18,000 or more.

The point here is that to totally defer taxable gain at the time of the exchange you must purchase a property with an equal or higher price than the property being sold. If you do not, the IRS will take the position that the first dollars taken out of the exchange represent capital gains or recapture of depreciation, and you will be fully taxed on the difference. That is why most people use like-kind exchanges to trade up in value.

How Do I Avoid Receiving Taxable Boot?

Remember from our discussion of the foundation of like-kind exchanges that the courts and the IRS agreed that for a delayed exchange to qualify for tax deferral the exchanger cannot receive any funds or other property from the sale of the relinquished property before he

receives the like-kind replacement property. This rule is so critical that any receipt
of boot, whether actual or constructive,
before receipt of the replacement property
may disqualify the entire exchange. At the
very least, it will disqualify a portion of the
sale proceeds that the taxpayer received.
Actual or constructive receipt means that
the exchanger has access to or control over
the funds or proceeds.

You will hear the term "boot" used to
refer to funds or proceeds that the exchanger
either has access to or control over. Boot is
an old English term meaning "something

**INCLUDE
ACQUISITION
EXPENSES
IN PURCHASE PRICE**

Acquisition expenses can be
included in the purchase price
of the replacement property.
This could include closing fees,
inspection fees, loan fees,
points, commissions, and all
other closing costs related to
the purchase.

given in addition to." In the case of like-kind exchanges, boot means the
money and fair market value of other property received by the taxpayer
in an exchange. Money includes all cash, cash equivalents, debts, liabilities, or mortgages of the taxpayer that are either assumed by another
party or are liabilities to which the property exchanged by the taxpayer
is subject. Other property is property that is not like-kind, such as personal property, a promissory note from the buyer, or a promise to perform work on the property.

The most common example of boot is cash taken away from the
exchange, especially in the case of trading down where the sale price of
the replacement property is less than that of the relinquished property.
There are many sources of taxable boot other than the net cash received
from the exchange. Below are common examples of noncash boot to be
aware of so that you do not inadvertently create taxable gain in a like-
kind exchange:

Debt reduction: Debt-reduction boot occurs when the taxpayer's debt
on the replacement property is less than the debt owed on the relinquished property. Like cash boot, debt-reduction boot can be avoided
by trading up instead of trading down in the exchange, or if you must
trade down, finding qualified expenses to offset the lower price of the
replacement property.

THE EXCHANGE AGREEMENT

In order for a qualified intermediary to meet the safe harbor requirements, there must be a written agreement between the taxpayer and the intermediary expressly limiting the taxpayer's right to receive, pledge, borrow, or otherwise obtain the benefits of money or other property held by the qualified intermediary.

Nonqualified expenses: Using sales proceeds to pay for costs other than qualified closing expenses will result in boot. Examples of nonqualified expenses include, rent prorations, utility charges, and tenant damage deposits transferred to the buyer. Bringing cash to the closing of the replacement property can help avoid the need to use sale proceeds for nonqualified expenses.

Excess borrowing: Borrowing more money than is necessary to close on the replacement property will likely result in boot. Taxpayers usually take the position that the loan acquisition costs are paid out of the loan proceeds; however, there is no IRS guidance on this issue, and it is possible the IRS could take the position that these costs are being paid with exchange funds. At any rate, it is best to limit borrowing to the amount necessary to acquire the replacement property.

Non-like-kind property: Not surprisingly, the value of any non-like-kind property received in the exchange will be treated as boot. It is best to avoid receiving non-like-kind property.

Who Is a Qualified Intermediary?

A qualified intermediary (also known as an *accommodator*) is an individual or entity that satisfies the safe harbor requirements of the IRS rules and regulations and can legally hold funds to facilitate a like-kind exchange. Since using a qualified intermediary creates a *safe harbor*, or legal presumption that the taxpayer has not actually or constructively received proceeds, virtually all like-kind exchanges today involve a qualified intermediary. The key is to hire the qualified intermediary before you close on the sale of the relinquished property. Once you close and receive funds, it is too late to decide to do a like-kind exchange.

Besides creating a safe harbor, using a qualified intermediary streamlines the exchange process and allows the taxpayer to focus on choosing the right replacement property. The qualified intermediary will prepare all of the necessary documents, hold the funds, and coordinate the exchange, including acquiring and transferring title to the properties involved in the exchange. Given the low cost of hiring a qualified intermediary, there really is not a good reason to not use one.

The IRS restricts certain persons from acting as qualified intermediaries. Basically, a qualified intermediary cannot be related to the taxpayer or have had a financial relationship with the taxpayer in the two years before the taxpayer relinquishes the property. This means the taxpayer cannot use her current attorney, certified public accountant, or real estate agent. In addition, corporations or other legal entities owned by disqualified individuals cannot be used as qualified intermediaries.

Not many states require qualified intermediaries to be licensed and there are no federal standards, so you need to choose carefully. It is best to use well-known intermediaries who have a lot of experience with like-kind exchanges and strong financial statements. It also makes sense to check that the qualified intermediary you choose is bonded and insured against errors and omissions and employee dishonesty.

> ### EXCHANGES WITH RELATED PARTIES
>
> Be careful with like-kind exchanges between related parties. The IRS does not like related parties as qualified intermediaries or as exchangers in like-kind exchanges. The IRS defines related parties as you and a member of your family (spouse, brother, sister, parent, child). Related parties also include you and a corporation or partnership in which you own more than 50 percent of the ownership interests, capital interests, or profits. If you do a like-kind exchange with a related party and either of you dispose of the exchanged property within two years, the exchange will be disallowed and the tax on the original exchange will be triggered as of the date of the later disposition. So if you do an exchange with a related party, you must hold the property for two years.

How Much Time Do I Have to Complete the Exchange?
There are two critical time limits for a like-kind exchange: a 45-day identification period and a 180-day exchange period. The identification period covers the time you have to identify replacement properties,

NEED MORE TIME?

Hopefully, before you officially put the relinquished property on the market you have begun thinking about replacement property. However, if you are having difficulty locating replacement property or the relinquished property sells faster than expected, try to negotiate a longer escrow period in the sales contract to give you more time to find adequate replacement property.

and the exchange period covers the time you have to close on the purchase of replacement property. The IRS does not grant extensions on these time limits! It is very important to understand the rules and then count and recount the days. Following is an explanation of the timing verbatim from the federal regulations:

➤ The identification period begins on the date the taxpayer transfers the relinquished property and ends at midnight on the 45th day thereafter.

➤ The exchange period begins on the date the taxpayer transfers the relinquished property and ends at midnight on the earlier of the 180th day thereafter or the due date (including extensions) for the taxpayer's return of the tax imposed by Chapter 1 of subtitle A of the Code for the taxable year in which the transfer of the relinquished property occurs.

The IRS is so serious about these time limits that they will not give you an extra day even if a deadline falls on Thanksgiving, Christmas, or New Year's Day. What if your identified replacement property is destroyed by fire or some other act of God after the expiration of the forty-five-day identification period? Sorry, you will not be given an extension to identify another property. Even mistakes cannot be corrected, for example, mistakenly using the wrong address to identify a property. Did we mention that there were no exceptions?

Despite strict enforcement of the time limitations in a 1031 transaction, there is some flexibility for identifying replacement properties. You are allowed to identify more than one replacement property. This gives you a little more time to perform the financial analysis needed to make a good investment decision, and it gives you options if something happens to take one of the properties off the market.

Regardless of the number of relinquished properties transferred as part of the like-kind exchange, the maximum number of replacement properties you can identify is controlled by two rules: the three-property rule and the 200-percent rule.

➤ Three-property rule: Any three properties regardless of their fair market values.

➤ 200-percent rule: Any number of properties as long as their aggregate fair market value as of the end of the identification period does not exceed 200 percent of the aggregate fair market value of all the relinquished properties as of the date the relinquished properties were transferred by the taxpayer.

What happens if you identify more replacement properties than permitted by the three-property rule and the 200-percent rule? The IRS will treat you as not having identified any replacement properties and you will not be able to complete the like-kind exchange! The IRS regulations offer some relief from this strict interpretation, and they will consider a satisfactory identification to be made with respect to:

➤ Any replacement property received by the taxpayer before the end of the identification period, and

➤ Any replacement property identified before the end of the identification period and received before the end of the exchange period, but only if the taxpayer receives before the end of the exchange period identified replacement property the fair market value of which is at least 95 percent of the aggregate fair market value of all identified replacement properties (the 95-percent rule).

It is surprising how often these alternative methods of identifying replacement property come up in practice. Clearly, the simplest route is to identify three replacement properties. If you cannot follow the three-property rule, seek an attorney or accountant or talk to your qualified intermediary to help you comply with these alternative rules.

Once you locate the replacement properties and figure out the timing, you need to formally identify the property. Yet another benefit of using a qualified intermediary is that this person will have a form to use for replacement property identification. The key is to provide enough information to adequately identify the particular property. A street address, legal description, or county parcel number should work. However, a street address for a building with one hundred condominiums is not specific enough. You would also need to identify the particular unit.

SPECIAL CIRCUMSTANCES

The basic strategy with like-kind exchanges is not too difficult to understand. Instead of selling a property and paying the taxes or purchasing another one, exchange your property for a like-kind property of equal or greater value so that your funds keep working for you and not the U.S. Treasury. As you exchange properties, however, you will likely come across unique situations. We discuss some of the most common unique situations in the following sections.

Combine Like-Kind Exchange with Installment Sale

Sometimes it makes sense to combine tax strategies. One example that can work well is combining a like-kind exchange with an installment sale. For more on installment sales see Chapter 6. By combining the two strategies you can step down to a smaller investment property and still defer taxable gains. You can also diversify your investments between real estate and holding a promissory note. In Chapter 6, we discuss the impact of combining these two strategies on the treatment of the installment sales part of the transaction. There can be some tricky issues that pop up when combining these two strategies, depending on whether the properties are mortgaged and the timing of the exchanges. Effectively combining these strategies will require consultation with your tax advisor.

Investment Property or Primary Residence?

In Chapter 5, we discuss how the primary residence exclusion exempts the first $250,000 of taxable gain for an individual and $500,000 for a married couple on the sale of their primary residence. Imagine the tax savings possibilities of deferring taxes with a like-kind exchange and then eliminating the taxable gain altogether by converting the property to a personal residence and qualifying for the primary residence exclusion when you sell. This is possible.

However, current IRS rules make it more difficult. Basically, the current rules require a taxpayer to hold the 1031 replacement property for at least five years and use it as an investment property for part of the time. Then the taxpayer still must use the property as his main residence for at least two more years before selling it.

> **DO NOT FORGET ABOUT RECAPTURE OF DEPRECIATION**
>
> When the investment property is a rental, do not forget to figure recapture of depreciation into your financial analysis. While the rental may be converted to a primary residence and avoid capital gains tax treatment, you cannot avoid taxes due as a result of recapturing any depreciation taken on the property when it was an investment.

Example: Barry uses a like-kind exchange to trade a four-unit apartment building on which he has $300,000 of taxable gain for a $600,000 single-family home replacement property that he plans to rent for cash flow and appreciation. By using a like-kind exchange, he avoids paying $45,000 in taxes (assuming a 15 percent rate). He rents the property for five years. After the lease expires he decides he would like to move his family into the house and use it as their primary residence. Barry lives in the house for two years and decides to sell it. The house is now worth $700,000. Assuming his basis in the property at the time of the sale is still $300,000, Barry will have a gain of $400,000. However, he will likely owe nothing in taxes because he and his wife now qualify for the $250,000/$500,000 primary residence exclusion. Not a bad result!

The IRS looks at the taxpayer's intent in this type of situation to determine whether the property is held for investment. Specifically, what was the taxpayer's intent at the time of the exchange? Was it investment or was it to eventually move into the property as a primary residence? If the IRS determines Barry's intent at the time of acquiring the replacement property was to use it as a primary residence, his like-kind exchange will likely be disqualified. A red flag to the IRS is a relatively short time period during which a replacement property is rented and the time the taxpayer begins to use the property as his primary residence. If Barry has documentation that he was analyzing the replacement property for investment purposes, this would be helpful to establish his intent that the replacement property was purchased as an investment, not a primary residence.

The bottom line is that it is possible for a property to qualify for a like-kind exchange and the primary residence exemption. However, this is a touchy area and you should work with your tax advisor if you plan to implement this strategy.

Vacation Property or Investment?

On the flip side, there are times when it may be best to change your use of a property to qualify it as property held for use in a trade or business or for investment purposes in order to qualify it for 1031 treatment. This issue often arises when a person decides to sell a vacation property. The question is whether you have been using the property for personal use or as an investment.

If you rented your property for more than fourteen days during the year at a fair rental rate and used it personally for less than the greater of fifteen days or 10 percent of the number of days during the year it was rented at a fair rental rate, it is likely an investment. Otherwise, it is probably not an investment. And if you reported rental income and deducted rental expenses for the property on your tax return, then it looks like you are holding the property for investment purposes. On the other hand, if you claimed a second-home mortgage deduction for the property, then it looks more like a vacation home held for personal use.

Remember, the IRS will look at all the facts and circumstances, including your treatment of the property on previous tax returns. To recharacterize the property for a like-kind exchange you may need to take actions like listing the home with a rental agent and/or online vacation rental listing service and treating it as an investment property on your tax return, including showing rental income and expenses.

Keep in mind that the replacement property in a like-kind exchange must also be held for investment. So if you are going to exchange one vacation property for another, both properties must be held for investment purposes. An IRS audit will look at your intention at the time you made the exchange, so carefully document your investment intent.

Remember, the mere hope or expectation that a property will appreciate is not enough to classify it as being held for investment when the evidence overwhelmingly suggests the taxpayers use it as their personal vacation retreat. Following are some conservative guidelines for holding investment properties in a vacation or resort area:

> **QUALIFY YOUR VACATION HOME**
>
> By treating a property previously held for personal use, like a vacation home, as an investment property for at least two years you can potentially qualify the property for a like-kind exchange.

➤ Keep personal use incidental, generally less than the greater of fifteen days per year or less than 10 percent of the time rented at fair market value.
➤ Rent or attempt to rent the property for two years.
➤ Deduct mortgage interest as an investment interest expense, not a home mortgage interest expense.
➤ Take all possible tax benefits associated with investment property, including deductions for maintenance expenses.
➤ Include rental income on your tax return.

Reverse Exchanges

In a typical like-kind exchange, the taxpayer relinquishes the old property and then goes about trying to identify a replacement property. There are times when this sequence of events will not work out and you will need to reverse the sequence. Thankfully, in these cases you may be able to complete a reverse exchange. As the name indicates, it is just the opposite of a forward exchange: the taxpayer acquires the replacement property prior to transferring the relinquished property. Reverse exchanges are considerably more sophisticated, complex, and expensive than a typical deferred exchange; however, there are situations where doing a reverse exchange is worth the time and expense, including:

➤ The transfer of the relinquished property is delayed or otherwise falls apart.
➤ The taxpayer identifies an irresistible good deal on a replacement property and must move quickly.

REVERSE EXCHANGES ARE EXPENSIVE

Careful planning needs to precede use of a reverse exchange. Given the newness and the formalities involved, the costs can be high. Unlike a traditional like-kind exchange, which normally costs between $500 to $750, the cost of a reverse exchange can be around $5,000.

➤ The taxpayer chooses to search and find the perfect property and arrange for its purchase prior to transferring the relinquished property.

➤ The taxpayer desires to build the replacement property (this type of build-to-suit exchange, whether typical or reverse, can be risky due to potential construction delays).

Reverse exchanges are fairly new. The IRS authority to complete a reverse exchange comes from a September 2000 revenue procedure that addressed what some call parking arrangements and specifically allowed reverse exchanges under certain circumstances. A parking arrangement occurs when the taxpayer arranges with a friendly party to buy and hold the desired replacement property while the taxpayer sells the relinquished property. Once the relinquished property is sold the exchange is completed by the taxpayer acquiring the replacement property from the friendly party.

Revenue Procedure 2000-37 created new terminology and formal rules for this "friendly" parking arrangement. The person buying and holding the replacement property is called the *exchange accommodation titleholder* (EAT or AT). The relationship between the EAT and the taxpayer/exchanger is formalized in a *qualified exchange accommodation arrangement* (QEAA). An EAT is usually just the qualified intermediary you select, and a qualified exchange accommodation arrangement is simply a written agreement between the taxpayer and the EAT setting out the requirements specified in Revenue Procedure 2000-37. The QEAA must meet a number of requirements, including: (1) title to the replacement property must be held by someone other than the taxpayer or a disqualified person, and (2) the combined time period that the properties are held in the QEAA cannot exceed 180 days.

Co-Ownership and Partnership Challenges

Investment real estate is commonly owned by co-owners, sometimes as tenants in common and sometimes in a partnership or limited liability company. A tenant-in-common interest does not pose a problem for like-kind exchange eligibility if managed correctly. See Chapter 8 for more about like-kind exchanges and tenant-in-common interests. However, a partnership interest cannot be exchanged in a 1031 transaction, and limited liability companies are commonly treated as partnerships for federal tax purposes.

If the partnership desires to complete a like-kind exchange by selling a property and taking title to the replacement property in the name of the partnership, there would not be a problem. Frequently, however, the partners may want to discontinue the partnership, sell the property, and go their separate ways. This situation presents a challenge and requires careful planning, and even then it is not without tax risk.

Generally, the partnership must distribute deeded tenant-in-common interests to the partners. Then the former partners must hold the tenant-in-common interests for some period of time before engaging in a 1031 transaction to satisfy the held-for requirement of a like-kind exchange. This strategy is helpful when one or more partners want out of the partnership but the remaining partners wish to engage in a like-kind exchange. In this case, only the departing partners would receive the distribution of tenant-in-common interests.

This strategy has some risk because the IRS, to our knowledge, has not provided any guidelines for how long the tenant-in-common interests must be held after being distributed before they qualify for a like-kind exchange. Tax advisors differ about how long the tenant-in-common interests must be held before a like-kind exchange. Some say no significant holding time is necessary.

When Not to Use a Like-Kind Exchange

It may be hard to believe, but there are times when a like-kind exchange may not make sense, even if you have a replacement property. One of those times may be when you have a loss. A like-kind exchange will defer losses just as it will defer taxable gain. If you will incur a loss on a property and can use it to offset other gain or income, then it will likely make more sense to just sell the property and take the loss.

CLOSING NOTES ON LIKE-KIND EXCHANGES

A like-kind exchange allows a real estate investor to defer the payment of taxes. This in turn allows the investor to keep and reinvest otherwise taxable profit, which results in accelerated wealth accumulation. The general rule is that no gain or loss shall be recognized on the exchange of property held for productive use in a trade or business or for investment if such property is exchanged solely for property of like-kind that is to be held either for productive use in a trade or business or for investment. Here are a few final notes to close this chapter.

➤ In a deferred like-kind exchange, the taxpayer's sales proceeds are received and held by a qualified intermediary.

➤ To fully avoid paying taxes on the exchange, the replacement property must be equal to or of greater value than the relinquished property.

➤ The two critical time restrictions are that the taxpayer must identify the possible replacement properties within forty-five days of the closing and buy the replacement property within 180 days of the closing.

➤ You can identify any three replacement properties regardless of value or any number of properties as long as the aggregate fair market value is not more than 200 percent of the aggregate fair market value of the relinquished property.

➤ There are restrictions on like-kind exchanges between family members.

➤ Any proceeds or other property received at the closing of the replacement property will be taxable boot. Taxable boot can include reduction of debt.

➤ It is possible to convert an investment property acquired in a like-kind exchange into a primary residence and take advantage of the $250,000/$500,000 primary residence exclusion.

➤ It is also possible to convert a vacation home used primarily for personal use into an investment property for the purposes of a like-kind exchange.

➤ A reverse exchange enables a real estate investor to complete a like-kind exchange when the replacement property is identified before the relinquished property is closed.

➤ Partnership interests, limited liability interests, and other securities are not eligible for like-kind exchange treatment. To enable individual owners to engage in a like-kind exchange, distribute property out of the entity and hold it as tenants-in-common.

➤ The tax deferral, and potential tax elimination, that can be achieved when you follow the like-kind exchange rules carefully and trade up to higher value properties can create more wealth in a few short years than many salaried jobs can in a lifetime.

CHAPTER 8

Use TICs to Defer Taxes

Opportunity is missed by most people because it is dressed in overalls and looks like work.

—Thomas Edison

At its most basic level, a tenancy-in-common is a form of holding title to real property when there are two or more owners. We covered this basic idea of tenancy-in-common in Chapter 1. The tenancy-in-common (TICs) interests that we are going to cover in this chapter are real property investments that expand the options available to investors, especially those using like-kind exchanges. TICs, as we discuss them here, really came on the scene as an alternative investment after a 2002 IRS revenue procedure established the premise that a TIC can be real property for the purposes of a like-kind exchange. TICs open the door to a whole new world of real estate investing, but there are special issues and risks that must be understood before you jump in.

WHAT IS A TIC?

Let's start by explaining what a TIC is not. A TIC is not an interest in a partnership, limited liability company, or other type of business entity. It is a form of shared ownership where each investor owns an undivided fractional interest in real property. As you will see when we discuss the 2002 IRS revenue ruling, this distinction between owning an equity interest in a business entity versus owning an interest in real property is critical for preserving the tax benefits of a TIC investment.

Typically a cotenancy interest will be expressed as a percentage interest in the entire property. If a specific percentage interest is not expressed, the presumption is that each party has an equal interest. A key characteristic of a TIC is the right to freely transfer, encumber, or convey this separate tenant-in-common interest—known as rights of alienation. These rights distinguish a TIC interest from an ownership interest in a partnership or other legal entity.

A tenant-in-common interest also typically comes with a right of partition. Partition is a legal right to cause an equitable division of the property. Although partition may be possible for a large tract of undeveloped land, the physical partition of a commercial or residential property is often impossible. Therefore, a partition right typically leads to a judicial sale of the property and a partition of the proceeds. Like the right of alienation, this right of partition is a key distinguishing feature of TICs.

There are two primary markets for TIC investments. One market is income-producing commercial properties with financially strong tenants, such as retail shopping centers and large class A office buildings. The typical tenant leases for these properties are called *triple-net* leases, which require the tenant to pay all real property taxes, insurance, and many of the operating expenses associated with the property. These high-value commercial properties are too expensive for most individual investors to purchase outright. Another big market is rental real estate in resort areas; think Vail, Colorado. Again, this enables ownership by a group of investors who otherwise could not afford to buy these very expensive rental units and who need professional management since they may not live near the property.

Most TICs, in addition to being a real estate investment, are securities that are regulated by the Securities and Exchange Commission. A sponsor will acquire a rental property, find a tenant and put together the leasing arrangement (if necessary), fractionalize the property into tenancy-in-common interests, and then promote and sell those interests to raise funds for the investment. TIC interests that are securities (which are the vast majority) must be sold through a licensed securities broker dealer; a real estate license does not permit a real estate agent to sell federally regulated securities. An investor's return will be largely dependent on the strength of the leasing arrangement.

While a particular co-ownership structure may be treated as a tenancy-in-common under state real property laws, federal tax law may lead to different treatment. Co-ownership could be viewed by the IRS as a general partnership even if there is no written partnership agreement. Partnership interests do not qualify for like-kind exchange treatment. The determination is fact specific; just because a property is maintained, repaired, and rented, that does not make it a separate entity for federal tax purposes. However, a separate entity, like a partnership, may be created when:

➤ The co-owners or their agents perform services such as arranging financing, collecting rents, preparing statements, and purchasing and leasing equipment;

➤ The co-owners' ability to sell, lease, or encumber the property is limited; and

➤ The co-owners share profits and losses from the property with the manager or agent.

Providing customary services to tenants is okay, but the more extensive the activities and the more the venture looks like a business enterprise, the more likely a co-ownership will be treated as a partnership for federal tax purposes. This fact-specific analysis does not instill much confidence in a TIC investor.

REVENUE PROCEDURE 2002-22

In 2002, the IRS issued guidance in Revenue Procedure 2002-22 on whether an undivided fractional interest would be considered real property or an interest in a business entity (typically a partnership) for federal tax purposes. The difference is critical for the purposes of a like-kind exchange. If a TIC is treated as an interest in a business entity, then it does not qualify as like-kind real property for purposes of a like-kind exchange. Remember from Chapter 7 that like-kind property essentially means that real property must be exchanged for real property.

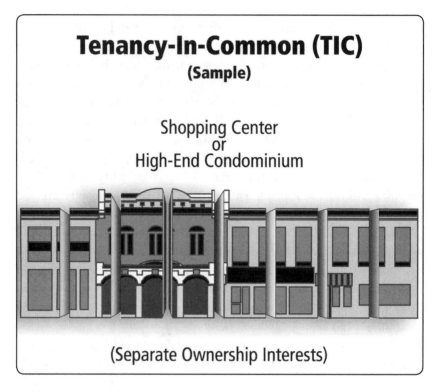

FIGURE 8.1 Tenancy-in-common

Although the IRS did not offer a definitive answer on this question, it did give us something to go on. The revenue procedure provides a set of fifteen conditions that taxpayers must meet before they can seek an advance ruling from the IRS on a particular TIC arrangement. A favorable ruling by the IRS would dispel the ambiguities, but most taxpayers do not wish to incur the cost or delay necessary for the IRS to issue a ruling on their particular situation. Instead, many taxpayers choose to rely, in good faith, on the guidance offered in the revenue procedure.

Following is a summary of the fifteen conditions from Revenue Procedure 2002-22:

1. *Tenancy-in-common ownership.* Each co-owner must hold title to the real property (either directly or through a "disregarded entity,"

such as a single-member limited liability company) as a tenant in common under the applicable state law.

2. *Number of co-owners.* The number of co-owners cannot exceed thirty-five persons. A husband and wife are treated as a single person, as are all persons who acquire interests from a co-owner by inheritance.

3. *Not a business entity.* The co-ownership may not file a partnership or corporate tax return or otherwise hold itself out as a partnership or other form of business entity. The IRS will not be likely to issue a favorable ruling if the co-owners held their interests in the real estate through an entity and then transferred it to the individuals immediately prior to formation of the co-ownership.

4. *Co-ownership agreement.* The co-owners may only enter into a limited co-ownership agreement that may run with the land and complies with the conditions on voting and the rights of partition and alienation.

5. *Voting.* The co-owners must retain the right to approve the hiring of any manager, the sale or other disposition of the property, any leases of a portion or all of the property, or the creation or modification of a blanket lien on the property. While these actions require unanimous approval, other actions may be determined by co-owners holding more than 50 percent of the total undivided fractional interest in the property.

6. *Restrictions on alienation.* Subject only to a lender's restrictions under customary lending practices, each co-owner must have the right to transfer, encumber, and partition the co-owner's undivided interest in the property without the agreement or approval of any person.

7. *Sharing proceeds and liabilities upon sale of property.* If the property is sold, any debt secured by a blanket lien must be paid off and the remaining sales proceeds must be distributed to the co-owners.

8. *Proportionate sharing of profits and losses.* All revenues generated by the property and all costs associated with the property must be shared in proportion to the co-owner's pro-rata undivided interests in the property.

9. *Proportionate sharing of debt.* The co-owners must share in any indebtedness secured by a blanket lien in proportion to their undivided interests.

10. *Options.* A co-owner may issue an option to purchase his undivided interest (a call option) provided that the exercise price reflects the fair market value of the property at the time the right is exercised. A co-owner may not acquire an option to sell the co-owner's undivided interest (a put option) to the sponsor, a lessee, another co-owner, the lender, or any person related to those parties.

11. *No business activities.* The co-owners' collective activities must be limited to those customarily performed in connection with the maintenance and repair of rental properties.

12. *Management and brokerage agreements.* The co-owners may enter into management or brokerage agreements with an agent as long as they are renewable no less frequently than annually. The agent may be a sponsor or a co-owner but may not be a lessee. Management fees cannot be based on the income or profits derived by any person from the property and may not exceed the fair market value of the manager's services.

13. *Leasing agreements.* All leasing arrangements must be bona fide leases, and the rents must reflect fair market value.

14. *Loan agreements.* The lender may not be related to any co-owner, the sponsor, the manager, or any lessee.

15. *Payments to sponsor.* The amount paid to the sponsor for the acquisition of the co-ownership interest or for any services rendered by the sponsor must reflect fair market value. In addition, such payments cannot be based on income or profits derived by any person from the property.

There are many nuances and complexities to these guidelines. This is definitely an area where you should talk to a qualified tax and legal advisor before establishing a tenant-in-common arrangement or investing in one to be sure that it will accomplish your goals, which will likely include the ability to qualify for a Section 1031 like-kind exchange.

WHAT ARE THE RISKS?

Whether you are sponsoring a TIC or investing in one, it requires significant due diligence. The vast majority of TICs are considered securities for federal law purposes, which means that the promoter is required to provide substantial investment disclosures to comply with federal securities laws. There is some irony with the treatment of TICs as both securities for federal securities law purposes and real property for federal tax purposes.

Another consequence of being a security under the securities laws is that most TICs are only sold to accredited investors. An accredited investor, for the purposes of federal securities law, is generally a person whose individual net worth or joint net worth with a spouse exceeds $1 million or who has income in excess of $200,000 ($300,000 if joint with spouse) in each of the two most recent years and who expects income in excess of that amount in the current year.

The goal behind the securities laws is to protect individuals who are not capable of evaluating and affording the risks of an investment. Owning real estate through a tenant-in-common arrangement comes with all the standard risks of owning real estate and securities, and some unique risks.

Offering Materials

Before you can manage a risk as an investor you need to understand the risks associated with a particular investment, and the best way to do this with a TIC is to carefully review the offering materials related to any tenant-in-common investment. The benefit of being a security is that significant disclosure is required. Virtually all the information you need about the investment and the property should be readily available, including the following facts.

➤ *Property*: Location, market demographics, zoning classification, improvements, construction history, inspection reports, financing documents, encumbrances, environmental issues, current appraisal, and property tax records.

➤ *Ownership*: Number of co-owners and any tenancy-in-common agreement.

➤ *Leases and tenants*: Tenant financials, rent rolls, lease and any sublease agreements.

➤ *Return on investment*: Potential income stream, timing of payments, typical and projected expenses, debt financing arrangements, depreciation schedule, and expected holding period.

➤ *Management team*: Existing management team, relationship to sponsor, and management agreements.

You will also want to check the background of the sponsor and broker involved in the promotion and selling of the TIC. Also be sure to have your tax and legal advisor review any offering materials.

Illiquid Investment

Most real estate is an *illiquid* investment, meaning it cannot be quickly and easily converted into cash. During the last decade, many investors had forgotten this fact. The last few years has reminded most everyone owning real estate that cycles are inevitable. Still, illiquid is relative.

If you own a property by yourself, illiquid basically means that there is no guarantee that a property will sell within any specific period of time. However, you can unilaterally make the decision to put it on the market and at least try to sell it. If you own an undivided fractional interest in a property or a TIC, selling your interest may require the cooperation of the other owners and be subject to additional conditions and fees.

Of course, you may be free to sell your undivided interest without anyone's approval, but there is not a well-developed secondary market for TIC investments at this time. It is possible that another co-owner would purchase your interest or that the sponsor could find a buyer for your interest, but the reality is that you should plan to hold a TIC at least through the anticipated holding period established for the investment. Most TICs have business plans that contemplate owning the property from three to ten years, and you need to inquire about this time frame before you invest.

You may have a limited option to sell your individual TIC interest, but you will have no individual right to sell the underlying property. This can make a TIC investment especially illiquid.

Fees and Costs

The sponsor's up-front fees and closing costs (sometimes called load) can be high enough to impact the tax benefits and return on investment. In fact, in some cases they may even outweigh the benefits you would receive by qualifying for a 1031 transaction. The fees must be paid up-front at closing because Revenue Procedure 2002-22 prohibits sponsors from receiving payments that depend on the income and profits from the property. The sponsor incurs a lot of cost in conducting property due diligence, arranging financing, preparing the TIC investment, and complying with the tax and securities laws. The broker who sold the investment will also receive a commission. Be sure to uncover all of the fees and costs and include them when you calculate your anticipated investment return.

Management Control

To many people, the most attractive feature of a TIC is that they do not have to deal with the day-to-day management responsibility associated with owning a rental property. Not having to deal with property management relieves a lot of stress and frees the investor to consider properties that are not geographically close to his home. Some investors may find themselves uncomfortable with this lack of sole control, especially when you also consider that many of the big decisions (such as hiring a manager) require a unanimous vote of the co-owners. In most cases, the co-owners will be widely dispersed and anonymous to you, but you should be able to assess the quality of the property management team before you invest.

Change in Tax Status

The tax benefits of TICs hinge on whether they are characterized by the IRS as an interest in real property or an equity interest in a business entity such as a partnership. Not all TICs qualify as like-kind real property for purposes of a like-kind exchange. An unfavorable tax ruling made after you acquire a TIC interest in a like-kind exchange could be a tax disaster because it could trigger deferred taxable gain, recapture of depreciation, and even penalties. It makes sense to look for TIC arrangements that have received a favorable advance ruling from the IRS under Revenue Procedure 2002-22 (referred to as a private letter ruling) or that have a tax opinion from a qualified law firm that the TIC qualifies for a 1031 exchange.

TICS AND LIKE-KIND EXCHANGES

As discussed previously, properly structured TICs can qualify for a tax-free like-kind exchange. The process is the same as for standard like-kind exchange. You simply identify a TIC as a possible replacement property within the forty-five-day identification period. The nice thing about TICs is that most are marketed with a set closing date so you can comply with the timelines of the 1031 transaction. For this reason, identifying a TIC can be a nice backup if the other identified properties fail to close. Of course, a TIC can also be the relinquished property in a 1031 transaction.

The deferred capital gains tax and depreciation recapture that can be accomplished through a 1031-TIC investment can preserve a significant amount of wealth, but there are other tax advantages as well. If the underlying property has existing nonrecourse debt financing, you may be able to increase your basis, which could provide additional depreciation deductions to shelter your rental income. TICs are often leveraged with 50–75 percent nonrecourse debt financing. The depreciation pass-through and interest deductions can partially shelter your portion of the rental income from income taxes.

CLOSING NOTES ON TICS

Many investors desire the passive income offered by TICs—a steady stream of income without the hassles of day-to-day property management. This income may be partially tax sheltered with available deductions similar to other real estate investments. In addition, TICs enable you to own an interest in real estate that otherwise would be cost prohibitive to own alone. However, TICs are subject to special risks and fees that can impact your investment decisions and results. Here are a few more notes about TICs to close this chapter.

➤ TICs that comply with Revenue Procedure 2002-22 are likely to be treated as interests in real property that qualify for a tax-free like-kind exchange, and it is best to acquire TICs that have a private letter ruling or opinion letter on this matter.

➤ An unfavorable ruling by the IRS after you acquire a TIC in a 1031 exchange could be bad news, triggering taxable gain and recapture of depreciation deferred in prior like-kind exchanges, and even penalties.

➤ Most TICs involve very little management by the co-owners, which can be good for taxpayers interested in reducing or eliminating property management duties.

➤ TICs are illiquid investments, so you need to carefully review the offering materials, ask about available exit strategies, and plan to hold for the long term.

PART THREE

Identify and Reduce Risk

CHAPTER 9

Asset Protection Basics

The availability of private insurance provides tremendous insulation for millions of individuals.

—Lawrence Summers

A re you a target for a lawsuit? You probably think that the real targets are the dot-com billionaires or the Donald Trump-type real estate developers. While the super wealthy are certainly at high risk of being sued, they can easily afford to fight lawsuits, and that in itself can be a deterrent. Imagine someone with a small fortune of, say, a million dollars spending $50,000 in legal fees to defend a case and then losing half of his fortune in court. Suddenly this person's financial security and retirement scenario have dramatically changed. The harsh reality is that many of the civil lawsuits filed every day in America target small business owners and individuals with less than $1 million in net worth. The best way to protect yourself is to take advantage of some or all of the strategies we discuss in this chapter and the following chapter to make yourself an unattractive lawsuit target and to limit your exposure if you do become a target.

THE RISKS

Before we discuss how to protect yourself and your real estate assets, you need to understand the risks. The most common threats come from:

➤ Lawsuits
➤ Creditors
➤ Bankruptcy
➤ Disasters

PROHIBITED TRANSFERS

Asset or fund transfers by a debtor that occur within ninety days of a bankruptcy filing can be set aside by the trustee. It is assumed these transfers are done to avoid creditors. Transfers to insiders, such as relatives, may be voided if they occur within one year of the bankruptcy filing. Any asset or fund shifting to a spouse or someone else for asset protection purposes should be done before there are any signs of a possible bankruptcy.

Lawsuits

Most people think of personal tort liability when they think of lawsuits. These are the classic slip-and-fall cases where someone is injured slipping on a patch of ice in front of a rental property. However, tort liability is only one of three primary sources of potential liability. (See Figure 9.1.) There is also liability in contract, for example, when someone serves as a guarantor on a bank loan or defaults on the terms of a real estate purchase contract. And then there is vicarious liability, which makes you liable for the actions of another person. For example, parents can be held responsible for the actions of their minor children. The time and money spent defending lawsuits can be the same no matter if the claim is legitimate or frivolous.

Creditors

Creditors have their own legal recourse for getting the money they are owed. Creditors with legitimate claims are usually awarded a judgment by the court. They then collect on this judgment with a writ of execution. The writ allows a sheriff or other law enforcement officer to seize and sell tangible personal property of the debtor to satisfy the obligation. If the debtor owns real estate, the judgment can be recorded by the creditor in the county where the real estate is located. This results in a lien against the real estate. The creditor can then foreclose the lien and force a sale of the property. If the debtor is a limited liability company or certain type of partnership, the creditor may be able to charge the interest of a member or partner and intercept distributions made to the member or partner. If the debtor is a corporation, the creditor may be able to gain full possession and rights to the debtor's shares of stock.

Bankruptcy

In the worst of cases, the debtor becomes insolvent. When you have more liabilities than assets, federal bankruptcy protection may be available under Chapters 7, 11, 12, or 13 of the federal bankruptcy code. Most states exempt certain assets from being taken in a bankruptcy. All other assets, known as nonexempt assets, become part of the bankruptcy estate and are under the control of a bankruptcy trustee. These nonexempt assets are normally used to repay creditors to some extent.

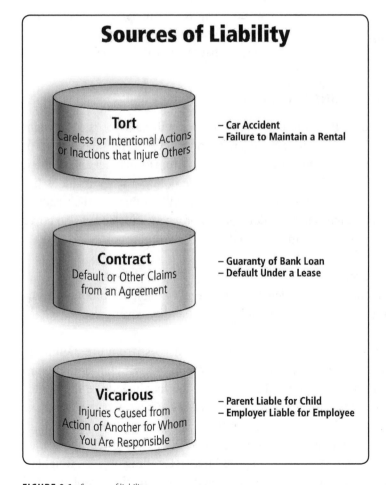

FIGURE 9.1 Sources of liability

DO NOT FORGET TO COVER LEGAL FEES AND COSTS

The expense of retaining competent legal counsel can be significant. Proper insurance coverage should include amounts for a legal defense against the claims made against you as the owner of the real estate.

Disasters

Even if you have been lucky and avoided lawsuits and kept your financial affairs under control and avoided creditors, there are some things that are completely beyond your control. A disaster, such as a fire or hurricane, can wipe out real estate faster than any other type of risk. Who can forget the images of hurricane-ravaged New Orleans? What you can do, however, is understand the degree of risk based on the property's location and properly insure against that risk.

INSURING AGAINST RISKS

Understanding the available policy options will help you ask the right questions. Typical insurance coverage for real estate protects you from losses caused by many dangers, including fire, storms, personal injury, burglary, and vandalism. A comprehensive policy usually includes liability insurance for injuries or losses suffered by others as the result of defective or dangerous conditions on the property and should also cover the legal cost of defending personal injury lawsuits.

Basic Coverage

There are three basic levels of coverage available for property insurance policies, all of which should include liability coverage.

1. *Basic coverage*: Insures a property against loss from fire, lightning, explosion, windstorm or hail, smoke, riot or civil commotion, vandalism, and sprinkler leakage. It often does not include certain building contents, such as machinery and HVAC systems, unless these things are added as endorsements.
2. *Broad-form coverage*: Insures against the basics listed above plus protects against losses from glass breakage, falling objects, weight of snow or ice, water damage associated with plumbing problems, and certain collapses.

3. *Special-form coverage*: This is the broadest available coverage and covers your property against all losses except those specifically excluded from the policy. Obviously, this high level of protection is more expensive.

> **RESEARCH PREMIUMS BEFORE BUYING THE PROPERTY**
>
> Insurance premiums are based on the location, age, type, and quality of construction of your property. It is smart to get an estimate of the premiums before you buy a property to avoid the surprise of high premiums.

If you suffer a loss and need to make a claim, there are typically two ways an insurance policy could quantify how much it will pay for the loss.

➤ *Replacement cost*: This is the actual cost of replacing the damaged or destroyed property without subtracting for any physical depreciation.
➤ *Actual cash value*: This pays the cost of replacing the property after taking into account physical depreciation.

Actual cash value is normally less than the replacement cost. Most standard policies provide for actual cash value coverage only. Replacement cost coverage usually requires a specific endorsement and costs more. In our experience, replacement cost coverage is the better option and worth any additional cost. Replacement cost coverage will fully replace a property destroyed in a disaster. Actual cash value may not provide for full replacement without additional money from the owner.

Re-evaluating your insurance coverage on a regular basis is a good idea and is a must if your circumstances have changed. For example, a primary residence may be converted into a rental investment. Before a conversion, the owner should contact his insurance agent and convert his homeowner's policy to a landlord's policy that contains the special coverage riders not typical in a homeowner's policy. Be sure you have the proper coverage for your investment property or you could have claims denied.

Umbrella Coverage and Other Options

Umbrella coverage, sometimes referred to as excess liability coverage, can be a cost-effective way to significantly increase your liability protection. This type of coverage is designed to work with your basic policies and provides both additional and wider coverage that goes beyond the limits of basic general liability insurance. An umbrella policy typically kicks in once a policyholder's primary policy limits have been exhausted. Umbrella policies are not that expensive. Annual premiums for $1 million of additional coverage can be as low as a few hundred dollars. An umbrella policy should be purchased from the same company that handles your underlying primary liability insurance.

For investment properties, especially rentals, several other types of insurance coverage may be necessary to adequately protect your assets. An issue unique to rental property that may need coverage is the loss of rent that results in your inability to pay the mortgage. In addition, the law places a lot of responsibility on landlords to maintain their property in a good and safe condition. And if your property is maintained or managed by employees, you are responsible for them and their actions. You may want to consider additional coverage for these situations.

Deductibles

Once you have chosen the proper insurance coverage, you need to consider the deductible for the policies (the amount you are required to pay out of pocket if there is a claim). Deductibles follow a simple financial equation: the higher the deductible, the lower your insurance premium. Most investors begin their real estate investing without a big cash reserve, so paying a higher premium for a lower deductible may seem necessary. As your financial ability to self-insure grows, evaluate whether you should have a higher deductible.

Average deductibles for small investment properties range from $500 to $1,000 while larger real estate investments can have deductibles of $5,000 to $10,000. If you own multiple investment properties, explore the possibility of having a single insurance policy that covers all your properties or having an aggregate deductible where a loss at any one of your properties could be used toward meeting the aggregate deductible.

MAXIMIZING EXEMPT PROPERTY

There are certain assets that are so protected by state law that creditors cannot touch them. While the details vary in each state, most states offer some protection for your primary residence, certain retirement accounts, and college savings accounts. A good asset protection plan should include a method for allocating resources to maximize the use of these exempt assets.

> **HOME MORTGAGE DEBT IS GOOD DEBT**
>
> Not only is the debt on your home typically the cheapest money you can borrow, but the homestead exemption shows how home mortgage debt can also be used to deter creditors.

Homestead Exemption

Homestead laws generally protect a certain amount of the equity in your home from general creditors, give a surviving spouse the right to occupy the home, and reduce property taxes on a home (the tax adjustment often is just for the poor and the elderly). We focus on how these laws are used to protect the equity in your home. To qualify, a property must be occupied as a home by the owner or his family.

Most states place a dollar limit on the equity that can be protected from creditors' claims and an acreage limit on the amount of property that can be protected. In states with dollar limits, creditors can only go after home equity that exceeds the limit. For example, in California the exempt amount is $75,000. So if you have a house worth $400,000 and a $325,000 mortgage, there is nothing available for creditors. A few states like Florida and Texas have an unlimited homestead exemption.

Note that this exemption only applies to general creditors like credit card companies or lawsuit judgments. The federal government always has a right to seize your assets to collect debts or taxes. And the lender who loaned you money to purchase your home will also be able to force a sale to collect that debt. Most homestead exemptions also do not apply to a mechanic's lien for repairs or improvements made to the home.

Retirement Plans

Retirement plans, like homes, are given a lot of legal protection. The recent Bankruptcy Abuse Prevention and Consumer Protection

Act of 2005 (effective October 17, 2005) expanded the protection of retirement assets in federal bankruptcy. Essentially, retirement funds are excluded from federal bankruptcy estates up to a certain limit. This broad protection covers most tax-qualified retirement plans, deferred compensation plans, and tax-sheltered annuity plans. Traditional and Roth IRAs (which workers fund and create themselves) are subject to an aggregate dollar limit of $1 million that is adjusted for inflation and may be increased if the bankruptcy judge determines it is in the interest of justice.

Unfortunately, outside of federal bankruptcy the fate of retirement assets is less secure. Each state has different laws regarding whether claims and judgments outside of bankruptcy may attach or garnish retirement assets. The type of claim, for example domestic relations orders, can determine the level of protection. Due to the differences in state laws and rollover issues at the federal level, some retirement plans may require additional planning to be protected from creditor claims.

College Savings Plans

One of the most tax-advantaged and common college savings plans used today is known as the 529 Plan. Each state sponsors a separate 529 Plan. The 529 Plans operate much like an IRA but are for educational expenses. The plan participant transfers money in a qualifying 529 Plan savings account and then it grows tax free. Assuming it is eventually applied toward a qualifying educational purpose, there is no tax due upon distribution.

In the case of bankruptcy, federal law excludes from the bankruptcy estate all contributions deposited toward a 529 Plan savings account for a beneficiary who is the child, grandchild, stepchild, or step-grandchild of the debtor as long as the deposits were made at least two years before bankruptcy was filed and don't exceed the maximum amount permitted per beneficiary for the program. If the contributions were made between one and two years prior to the bankruptcy filing, the assets may still be protected up to $5,000 per beneficiary.

Another plus of 529 Plans is that most state laws offer much clearer protection for these plans than they do for retirement plans. Currently twenty-seven states have passed statutes that protect 529 Plans from creditors' claims more generally, including claims that have been brought outside of bankruptcy proceedings. The exceptions are Illinois, Michigan, and California, which do not have creditor protection statutes for 529 Plans in place beyond what is mandated by federal law. In some states, like Colorado, the protection is limited to the state's own 529 Plan, and in others, like Florida, it extends to any 529 Plan.

CLOSING NOTES

The first step in any asset protection plan is to sit down and carefully identity the most probable risks for your circumstances based on your investments and activities. After identifying your risks and most likely liabilities, you should use this information to select proper insurance coverage and properly allocate funds and assets. Listed below are closing notes on insurance coverage and asset allocation.

➤ Be sure you understand what each of your insurance policies cover. Typical property insurance coverage protects you from losses caused by many dangers, including fire, storms, personal injury, burglary, and vandalism.

➤ A comprehensive policy usually includes liability insurance for injuries or losses suffered by others as the result of defective or dangerous conditions on the property and should also cover the legal cost of defending personal injury lawsuits.

➤ An umbrella policy can provide extra protection for minimal cost. Plus, check into other forms of additional coverage that make sense for your situation.

➤ Most states exempt certain assets from the reach of creditors, usually a portion of the value of your primary residence, certain retirement accounts, and college savings accounts. Come up with a financial plan for allocating funds to maximize the use of these exempt assets.

➤ Proper allocation could mean transferring certain assets to a spouse or increasing funding to exempt property like retirement plans or home equity. Remember, however, that every situation is different, and you should talk with your legal and tax advisors before making any dramatic transfers.

CHAPTER 10

Ownership Structures: Divide and Conquer

We are always saying "let the law take its course," but what
we really mean is "let the law take OUR course."

—Will Rogers

lthough shielding your real estate assets from all risk is impossible, choosing the right legal entity to operate your business or hold title to your real property can offer very effective protection against creditors' claims. One of the main goals of using different legal entities is to create a strong division between personal assets and liabilities and business or investment assets and liabilities. For example, you do not want a lawsuit judgment from a real estate investment that went awry to result in a lien on your house. While this chapter focuses on asset protection, we also keep in mind the tax treatment of each entity. Several forms of legal ownership and the tax treatment of each, including a sole proprietorship, a corporation, a partnership, and a limited liability company, are covered in the following sections.

SOLE PROPRIETORSHIP

A sole proprietorship is simply a business owned and run by one person (or for tax purposes a husband and wife). There are no legal filings necessary to organize this type of entity, no extra taxes to be paid, and no hassles with other owners or partners. The major downside for the sole proprietor is that he is personally liable for everything since there is no legal difference between the individual and the business. While insurance can help reduce potential liability, if it fails, all of the owner's assets, whether personal or for use in the business, can be wiped out by creditors and judgments. Needless to say, a sole proprietorship is almost never the best choice for investing in real estate or operating a business since it does not offer any asset protection.

CORPORATION

A corporation certainly sounds much safer than a sole proprietorship, and it is, but it is still not usually a good choice for holding title to real estate. Corporations are treated as separate legal persons and can sue, borrow money, incur debt, and operate a business on their own behalf. Owners of the corporation receive shares of stock. While this legal separation offers a good deal of protection to your personal assets in the event of corporate wrongdoing, it is possible for a personal creditor to seize and sell your stock since the stock is a personal asset.

Despite this drawback, it is good to have a basic understanding of the two types of corporations for income tax purposes: a regular corporation (known as a C corporation) and a corporation that elects to be taxed under subchapter S of the Internal Revenue Code (known as an S corporation).

C corporations can receive many tax and fringe benefits. Plus, C corporations can usually accrue $50,000 of net earnings each year at the 15 percent federal tax bracket. However, C corporations are not pass-through (or conduit) tax entities; profits are taxed at the corporate level and again at the shareholder level as dividends or distributions (referred to as "double taxation"). So when your C corporation sells an appreciated property it will pay corporate-level taxes on the entire gain and then you will owe individual income taxes on any money distributed to you as a shareholder. This is why it virtually never makes sense to hold an appreciating investment or business property in a C corporation. These entities are really best for larger companies that want to raise capital by selling shares in the public markets.

The better option for small businesses is to elect S corporation status. By doing so, you eliminate the double taxation that exists with regular corporations. Income and losses maintain their character and pass through directly to you as the shareholder and are taxed at your individual income tax rate similar to partnerships. A tax advantage of S corporations that causes many business owners to use this type of entity is that distributions to shareholders are not subject to the self-employment tax (a 15.3 percent tax charged against your earned income up to a certain level that is used to pay Social Security and Medicare). Also, there may be opportunities with S corporations to shift or split income with family members who are in a lower income tax bracket.

> **REASONABLE SALARY**
>
> If you perform services for your S corporation you must pay yourself a reasonable salary (subject to self-employment taxes) in order to also pay yourself distributions that are not subject to the 15.3 percent self-employment tax.

A big problem with owning real estate through a corporation, either a C corporation or an S corporation, is that distributing appreciated real property to the owners triggers a taxable event.

> *Example:* Christina owns 100 percent of an S corporation. Years ago she used her S corporation to purchase a rental duplex in Maui for $300,000. Many years later she decided to retire to Maui, so she transferred title to one of the units (each unit has a fair market value of $500,000) into her personal name. Oops, the transfer is taxable. The taxable gain is calculated based on the fair market value of the property, which is much more than Christina's basis in the unit. If the basis in each unit was $100,000 at the time she made the transfer, she will owe income taxes of about $65,000. However, the worst part is that she received no cash from the transfer and so she will need to dip into her pocket to pay the taxes. If this transfer had occurred from a limited liability company or partnership (owned by Christina and her husband, Leonard), there would have not been a taxable event.

So if an S corporation is not ideal for holding real estate, can it be used in some way to take advantage of its tax benefits? Yes. As we mentioned, an S corporation is a great option for small businesses that can take advantage of the substantial savings in self-employment taxes by making distributions of dividends. Plus, combining an S corporation and a partnership or limited liability company can offer the best of both entities to real estate investors. For example, an S corporation can be used to run a property management business while a limited liability company can hold investment real estate. Income generated from the investment real estate could then be used to pay the management fees of the S corporation.

PARTNERSHIPS

From the previous discussion, you already know that an entity taxed as a partnership is one of the preferred methods of holding title to real estate. However, from a state law standpoint there are several types of partnerships, including limited partnerships, general partnerships, and limited liability partnerships. Some are much better than others from an asset protection perspective. A general partnership is essentially a sole proprietor plus at least one other person. It is the default classification for more than one person working together toward a common business purpose. A general partnership offers no liability protection and should be avoided.

A limited partnership, on the other hand, can offer pass-through (or conduit) tax treatment and legal protections. Limited partnership income simply flows through the entity to the individual partners and is taxed at the individual's ordinary income tax rate. Unlike the problem we saw with corporations, distributions of appreciated property can be made at its basis rather than its fair market value. This means there is flexibility to move assets around without triggering taxes.

Most state laws protect partnership interests from seizure and sale to satisfy personal creditors (unlike stock in a corporation). There is still, however, a liability problem with limited partnerships that involves the general partner. The business of a limited partnership is managed by a general partner who remains personally liable for the actions and debts of the business (unlike the management team in a corporation or limited liability company). Limited partners own part of the investment or business but do not participate in its operation, so they are given more legal protection from its activities. To reduce the personal liability of the general partner, it is possible to make the general partner a corporation or limited liability company.

This maneuver is not necessary in the many states that now have limited liability partnerships (and limited liability limited partnerships), which provide substantially the same legal protection as a limited liability company. These partnerships are created by filing the appropriate documents with the secretary of state just as with other legal entities.

Why use a limited liability limited partnership instead of a limited liability company? Limited liability limited partnerships may present the greatest possible chance for the use of tax savings valuation discounts when passing wealth from older members of a family to younger members of a family. These partnerships are sometimes referred to as family limited partnerships (FLPs) and can be such effective tools for owning and managing real property, reducing income and estate taxes, and providing management and estate planning options that we have dedicated a complete chapter to the subject (See Chapter 12). All things being equal, in most states and in most cases, the limited liability company is going to be the best entity for holding real estate.

LIMITED LIABILITY COMPANIES

Why is the limited liability company (LLC) the darling of tax advisors and attorneys? These entities combine excellent asset protection as well as conduit income tax treatment (that is, no double taxation). In addition, LLCs are incredibly flexible in the types and classes of membership interests that can be created and the available management structures.

LLCs can be slightly less difficult to organize than corporations and do not typically require legal formalities such as annual shareholder and director meetings. That said, we strongly encourage LLC owners to make a habit of formally approving important decisions of the LLC and even mimicking some of the formal requirements of a corporation. It does not take that much effort and can avoid disputes and provide helpful documentation if there is a dispute or a tax audit. The absence of certain legal formalities with an LLC means you cannot get into trouble for ignoring them; ignoring the legal formalities of a corporation, however, could result in a piercing of the corporate veil and personal liability.

An LLC is incredibly flexible in the way it can be organized and the types of membership interests that can be created, which can include

SINGLE-MEMBER LLCS VERSUS MULTIPLE-MEMBER LLCS

Single-member LLCs are not protected to the extent of multiple-member LLCs because a creditor may be able to take control of the LLC on the theory that the limitations imposed on a creditor with a charging order are unnecessary since there are no other members whose interests need to be protected.

interests that have preferred distribution rights. In most states, LLCs can also have any number and types of members, including foreign investors, corporations, other LLCs, and partnerships. Under the right circumstances, an LLC can even issue a profit interest to a member who will contribute future services (sweat equity) to the efforts of the business without any immediate tax consequences or required contribution of capital. This is not possible with a corporation.

When it comes to income taxation, an LLC is also a flexible entity. An LLC with two members is taxed as a partnership but can elect to be taxed as a corporation too. For purposes of holding real estate, it makes sense to elect to be taxed as a partnership for the reasons discussed previously (flow-through taxation and distributions at basis). A one-member LLC is treated as a sole proprietorship for tax purposes but still receives much of the liability protection afforded by the laws in the state in which it was organized.

Most significantly for the purpose of this chapter, an LLC is probably the best legal entity for protecting the assets of its members. Remember that if a corporate stockholder gets sued for any reason, the creditor can get control of the stock. Under most state laws, the only remedy for a creditor pursuing an LLC interest is to get a *charging order* directing that any distribution made to the member/debtor is paid to the creditor rather than the member. This is not a very satisfactory remedy for the creditor since he does not get the management and voting rights that go with the membership interest, and the LLC may choose not to make a distribution despite the fact that there is income. In the worst case, there may not be any income to distribute, and the creditor will have to wait a long time before the LLC earns enough to make a distribution.

There are a few legal questions that can arise in the formation of an LLC depending on the applicable state law.

➤ Some states require LLCs to terminate in thirty years or less.

➤ Some states require dissolution of an LLC on the death or resignation of a member, which can only be overcome by properly drafting the operating agreement.

➤ Some states require that an LLC have two or more members.

➤ Some states have special taxes on LLC income.

➤ Some states may create a variation in the asset protection and operation of the LLC, although this is much less true than it was even ten years ago since the laws are becoming more uniform.

Given all of the benefits to using an LLC, you should answer these questions under your state law before forming an LLC. It is also worth having an operating agreement carefully drafted for your particular situation since LLCs give you flexibility to structure them according to your wishes.

NEVADA AND DELAWARE

It is not uncommon to hear recommendations to form a corporation or limited liability company in another state, and Nevada and Delaware are often mentioned. While the reasons given for choosing these states vary, many people cite lower costs, tax savings, and stronger liability protection. Oftentimes these reasons are based on misconceptions or overzealous incorporating companies. It is almost always more cost effective to form your entity in your home state. And even though Nevada does not have a corporate income tax, you will need to go to the expense of filing a Nevada income tax return even if you do not live there.

It may make sense, however, to incorporate in a state other than your home state when you have a concern about an issue on which state law varies greatly. For example, there is a lot of variation in state law about when an individual can become personally liable for the debts and obligations of the legal entity (known as piercing the corporate veil). In many states, it is easier for this to happen than other states. In fact, the following states provide the least protection: California, Florida, Georgia, Louisiana, Texas, New York, and Pennsylvania.

One way the state variation comes into play is in capitalization requirements. A court can justify piercing the corporate veil and holding the owners personally liable if the organizers of the business did not meet the minimum capitalization (net assets) requirements of the state. There is typically no hard and fast rule for minimum capitalization requirements, which can vary for each situation. Case law in many states indicates that the minimum capitalization should be around $1,000, but Nevada case law holds it closer to $100.

In addition, many states will pierce the veil if the owners do not adhere to certain formalities, such as shareholder meetings, corporate minutes, and board of directors meetings. Nevada, on the other hand, has much more liberal standards and typically will not pierce the corporate veil because of a failure to comply with some of these legal formalities.

Another area where Nevada may address a unique concern is privacy. Shareholders in Nevada receive a higher degree of privacy than in many other states. For example, shareholders' names are not part of a public record. Nevada also does not require the disclosure of the company's principal business or the location of any offices outside of Nevada. Also, some commentators feel that Nevada is less willing than other states to share information about its corporations with other states, agencies, and governments.

Finally, Nevada law assigns only a pro-rata percent of responsibility to each individual who is found jointly liable for the debt of a company. This means that if a piercing of the corporate veil does occur, the entire liability cannot be assigned to a single shareholder, rather a particular percentage is assigned to each owner found liable for the judgment or debt. Many other states can assign the entire responsibility for the debt to a single owner notwithstanding the fact that he may not have been responsible for the entire obligation.

You might have also heard that it is smart to organize a business in Delaware. Delaware corporate law provides certain advantages, but it is geared more toward large, publicly traded corporations (like stringent corporate takeover laws). For most small businesses, including most that own or manage real estate, if you are not going to organize in your own state, Nevada is preferred because it offers a relatively greater degree of confidentiality and privacy as well as stronger protection against liabilities for stockholders, officers, and directors than many other states.

MULTIPLE ENTITIES

In our discussion of legal entities, it is important to note another strategy that we discuss with clients, especially those with higher-liability businesses or real estate investments. If one entity provides protection, we always ask whether more than one entity can

> **KEEP LIQUID ASSETS AWAY FROM OPERATING BUSINESSES**
>
> Given the high risks of business operations, you should not hold a large amount of liquid assets (cash and securities) in the same entity as an operating business.

provide additional protection. By separating out specific properties and sometimes even all properties into separate legal entities, each entity creates a firewall that protects its assets from the risks and liabilities of the other entities. This is because a liability created by an entity should only affect the assets owned by that entity (unlike a personal liability that could affect all the assets the person owns).

There are many ways to use multiple entities. One option is to create a separate entity for each investment. Another is to place projects in separate entities based on risk, segregating high-risk properties into separate entities. For example, if you own three rental properties and a piece of vacant land with a possible contamination issue, it may make sense to put the vacant land (and its potential environmental liability) into a separate LLC. That way in the event the environmental issue turns into a real liability, not only should the individual owners of the LLC be protected, but the three other rental properties should also be protected.

Multiple entities can also help to protect real estate from the liabilities that come from operating a business. Most liabilities occur as a result of operations rather than ownership (think employment lawsuits). For example, you own a ranch and board horses. One entity would hold title to the ranch property and another entity would run the boarding business. The entity that owns the real property would lease the ranch to the boarding business for one-year terms. If a customer's horse is injured in your stable and it results in a judgment, the only asset of the boarding business would be a leasehold for less than one year.

Another time when it may make sense to set up a separate entity is if you have a business that owns assets or does business in different states, especially aggressive states such as California that could assess penalties and interest for unpaid sales tax or other state-related income tax. By setting up a corporation or LLC just for the business conducted in the aggressive state, any past-due taxes or other liabilities arising from doing business within that particular state should be limited to the assets of that particular entity.

Of course, setting up and maintaining all of these entities can be expensive and time-consuming. Practically speaking, the average investor does not want to pay for or manage fifteen different entities for fifteen properties. Talk with your legal advisor to decide how many entities make sense for your assets and activities.

Several states, including Nevada and Delaware, have recently made this type of asset protection more cost-effective by allowing it to be done within one LLC known as a series LLC. The LLC laws in these states now provide for the creation of separate protected cells (each a series) within one limited liability container (the series LLC). The liabilities of a particular series are intended only to be enforceable against the assets of that series. There are certain formalities that must be satisfied to create this interseries liability protection. Because of state law variation and the newness of these entities, many lawyers are unsure about how this proposed liability protection would hold up in other states at this time.

TRUSTS

Trusts are mostly associated with estate planning and are discussed in Chapter 11. For the purposes of this chapter, trusts are just another type of entity that can provide some asset protection and tax advantages.

There are very specific rules about using trusts to protect assets from creditors. The general rule is that you cannot create an irrevocable trust for your own benefit that puts assets beyond the reach of creditors. State laws create variations on this general rule. For example, in Colorado there is an exception for cases where a solvent debtor puts assets in an irrevocable trust for the benefit of himself that cannot be reached by future creditors. Since the future creditors are not in existence at the time of the creation of the trust, the debtor is not evading his obligations or committing fraud.

You should also be aware that the federal bankruptcy laws were amended in 2005 to allow a trust to be voided by the bankruptcy trustee if the debtor made a transfer to a trust in which he is a beneficiary within ten years of filing the bankruptcy and there was an actual intent to hinder or defraud creditors. Arguably, there cannot be actual intent to defraud a creditor who does not exist at the time of the transfer, so this change in law would seem to have no effect on the previously mentioned Colorado law. Trusts created for tax-planning reasons should be even more secure from challenge because of a distinct motive to minimize taxes. The new bankruptcy law makes it critical to document your reasons for creating a trust.

OFFSHORE PLANNING

Offshore asset protection planning has received significant attention in the media. From our view there are a lot of effective asset protection techniques available here in the United States that are preferable due to the real and perceived risks involved in most offshore planning. Still, you may want to explore offshore options. Keep in mind that a taxpayer is responsible for reporting the existence of a foreign trust if she receives distributions from it or was the transferor to the foreign trust. One of the downfalls of this disclosure requirement is that it significantly increases the likelihood of an IRS audit.

In addition to increasing the chances of audit, there are a couple of other issues that should give you pause. One is that the initial expense and ongoing costs of managing offshore assets can be extremely high. There can also be a lot of uncertainty created by political unknowns with the foreign government where the assets are located and with how the U.S. government treats these assets. There have been some interesting federal court decisions dealing with offshore trusts that have resulted in jail time for the creators of the trust.

For example, in *FTC v. Affordable Media*, (nicknamed the Anderson case), a husband and wife, the Andersons, placed sales commissions from a telemarketing venture in a Cook Islands trust. The court ordered the Andersons to repatriate their trust assets, and they refused, claiming that they were unable to do so because the corporate trustee was prevented from returning assets in an event of duress. The court found the Andersons in contempt and ordered them taken into custody. Eventually the case was settled when the trustee paid the FTC $1.2 million, leaving the trust otherwise intact. If you choose to proceed with offshore planning, proceed with caution and realize that there may be some unexpected results.

CLOSING NOTES

In almost all cases, it is smart to own your assets or own your business through a properly organized legal entity. Asset protection, tax advantages, organizational formalities, and management rights are just a few of the issues that need to be considered when choosing an entity. Talk to competent legal and tax counsel prior to making a final decision. Following are a few final notes to take away from this chapter.

➤ C corporations are best for large business enterprises but are not good for owning real property since personal creditors can get control of the stock, and distributions of real estate to the shareholders can result in taxable gain. Plus, C corporation income is subject to double taxation.

➤ S corporations are best for small businesses because of the opportunity to save self-employment taxes. S corporations are not good for owning real estate because creditors can get control of the stock, and distributions of appreciated real estate to a shareholder can result in taxable gain.

➤ LLCs are almost always best for holding appreciating assets like real property and provide significant tax, operating, and management benefits.

➤ LLCs also provide good asset protection from personal creditors since creditors' remedies are limited to a charging order that only gives them the right to receive distributions that the owner of the membership interest would have received. The creditor has no management or voting rights in the LLC that may accompany the membership interest, and the managers of the LLC are free to decide not to make a distribution even if there is a profit.

➤ Partnerships are best when created as limited liability partnerships, which many states now allow. Limited liability limited partnerships (sometimes called family partnerships or FLPs) are useful for the management of family business and investment assets and for transfer tax and succession planning.

➤ A good practice is to use legal entities to insulate the potential liability of certain assets from other assets, including your personal assets.

➤ A business entity may be disregarded if it is set up purely to avoid taxes or defraud creditors and does not otherwise have a legitimate business purpose. A determined IRS or frustrated creditor may be able to convince a court to ignore the structure in the interests of justice. So keep it clean, follow all the necessary formalities, and document all of your decisions.

PART FOUR
Keep It in the Family

CHAPTER 11

Create a Legacy and Save Taxes

*The only thing you take with you when you're gone is what
you leave behind.*

—John Allston

Real estate is a significant component of many people's estates that
they—almost without exception—hope to pass on to their loved
ones with a minimum of hassle, expense, and confusion. Estate
planning with real estate and other assets has two primary goals: first, to
successfully give what you want to whom you want, at the time you want,
and in the manner you want; second, to effectively achieve goal one with
the lowest tax, legal, and administrative costs. Estate planning with real
estate presents a number of traps for the unwary but also many opportunities to minimize the tax and administrative costs often associated with
transferring assets from one generation to another.

BASIC PLANNING TECHNIQUES: TOOLS AND TERMS

To understand how real estate fits into the estate planning process, you
should have a basic understanding of the following terms and how they
work together: probate, wills, revocable living trusts, joint tenancy, pow-
ers of attorney, and gift and estate taxes.

Probate

Probate is a process by which a local court makes sure your debts are
paid and any assets you own in your sole name pass according to your
will or, if you don't have a will, according to state law. Assets owned in

> ### TITLING OF ASSETS IS IMPORTANT
>
> Beware: assets held in joint tenancy are not controlled by your will or trust. The only assets controlled by your will are those assets titled in your sole name and that do not have a beneficiary designation. Assets titled in a revocable trust can be administered without a probate.

joint tenancy with another person and assets with separate beneficiary designations (such as life insurance and IRAs) are not subject to probate. Probate can promote family harmony and imposes a time limit on creditors to make claims. However, probate can also tie up assets for six months to several years and can be expensive. Each state has different probate laws.

Revocable Living Trusts

A revocable living trust is a written agreement between a trustmaker (also called a settlor or a grantor) and a trustee (the manager of trust property for the benefit of the beneficiaries). Like a will, a revocable trust contains your instructions for the disposition of your assets after you die. During her lifetime, the trustmaker is most commonly also named as trustee and retains total control of the trust. A trust can be "funded" or "unfunded," depending on whether assets are transferred into it during the life of the trustmaker or after her death. If the trust is funded during the life of the trustmaker, assets titled in the name of the trust can pass to beneficiaries after the death of the trustmaker without being subject to probate. If the trust is unfunded, assets titled in the sole name of a deceased trustmaker will pass into the trust via the probate process and then be distributed to trust beneficiaries. Remember, assets owned in joint tenancy will not be controlled by your will or revocable trust but will pass directly to the surviving joint tenant by operation of law as discussed in Chapter 1.

Powers of Attorney

A financial power of attorney is a document granting one or more designated agents—usually close family members or trusted friends—the authority to transact business on your behalf if you are incapacitated and unable to make your own financial decisions.

Gift and Estate Taxes

The federal estate and gift tax, sometimes referred to as transfer taxes, are in flux. The *applicable exclusion*, an amount any one individual can pass to heirs estate tax free, is $2 million in 2008 and will increase to $3.5 million in 2009. In 2010, the estate tax is currently scheduled to be repealed. Sounds good so far, but the repeal is written to last only one year, and the current $1 million gift tax exclusion will remain. The current law reinstates the estate tax in 2011 with the applicable exclusion amount dropping back to $1 million. This nonsensical approach reminds us of the famous Will Rogers quote, "Every time they [Congress] make a joke, it is a law, and every time they make a law, it's a joke."

The estate tax can be especially harsh for very high-net-worth individuals who fail to plan to minimize its effect, because it can impose a maximum tax rate as high as 55 percent on estate assets. This is why proper estate planning is essential for high-net-worth individuals and anyone owning appreciating real estate.

Under current federal law, each person has a $1 million lifetime gift-tax exemption, meaning you can transfer up to $1 million of your assets during your life without a gift-tax liability. Gifts to your spouse (if he or she is a United States citizen) or to qualified charitable organizations are not subject to tax. In addition to a lifetime exclusion, you also have an annual exclusion, which allows you to transfer up to $12,000 (for 2008) to any individual that will not be subject to gift tax and will not impact your $1 million lifetime exclusion. For example, if you have two children, you can gift each child up to $12,000 in 2008—a total of $24,000 gift-tax free. If your spouse also makes similar annual exclusion gifts, you and your spouse can gift up to $48,000 in 2008 to the children. Any gifts to any one individual in excess of $12,000 will be applied to reduce your $1 million lifetime exemption.

ADVANCED PLANNING STRATEGIES WITH REAL ESTATE

High-net-worth individuals with estates in excess of the applicable exclusion amount or significant income should consider (with their tax advisor and attorney) one or more advanced real estate–specific tax planning strategies. We separate these strategies into family and charitable strategies.

Family Strategies

Strategies that keep assets in the family and minimize taxes are typically top estate planning priorities for real estate investors. For liquid assets, such as cash or marketable securities, making outright fractional gifts to adult family members is fairly easy and can accomplish the intended goals, but gifts of fractional interests in real estate cannot be so easily made.

Crummey Trusts

One relatively simple way to make annual gifts of fractional interests in real estate is through a so-called Crummey trust (named after the legal case that recognized the technique as viable). This form of trust allows the trust beneficiary to withdraw some or all of any contributions made to the trust for a period of time (which the contributor generally hopes the beneficiary will not do). As a result, some or all of the contributions will qualify for the gift-tax annual exclusion. Further, the trustee can have broad discretion over distributions of trust income and principal, and the trust need not terminate when the beneficiary reaches twenty-one.

The practical advantage of a Crummey trust compared to outright gifts is the donor need not fractionalize the real estate into separate shares for separate donees each year but can instead transfer a single share that can be kept intact under the management of a single trustee.

Qualified Personal Residence Trusts (QPRT)

A QPRT is an irrevocable trust drafted to own all or part of your primary residence or a vacation home. You reserve the right to reside in the residence for a term of years, and at the end of the term, ownership of the residence transfers to your children or other designated beneficiaries. The two primary tax benefits of the QPRT are that the gift-tax value of the transfer to the beneficiaries is determined at the time the QPRT is created (as compared to when the transfer of ownership to the QPRT beneficiaries is ultimately made when the market value of the residence may have increased) and that the fair market value of the gift to the QPRT beneficiaries is reduced by the value of your retained right to use the residence for the designated term.

Getting what you want in life often involves a tradeoff, and tax planning is no exception. In the case of lifetime gifts, such as QPRTs and other gifting techniques, taxpayers must balance the anticipated gift and estate tax savings of a particular planning technique against the lost capital gains tax savings had the same property passed to the same beneficiaries after the taxpayer's death. Because the highest gift and estate tax rates range from 35 to 55 percent and the long-term capital gain tax rate is currently 15 percent, the economic benefits of effective gift and estate tax planning usually trumps any loss of basis step-up. Analyzing these tradeoffs with your tax and estate planning attorney and CPA is appropriate before putting any particular tax planning strategy in place.

Grantor Retained Annuity Trusts (GRAT)

A GRAT is conceptually similar to a QPRT but can be used with any asset, not just a qualifying personal residence. For example, income-producing commercial real estate cannot be transferred to a QPRT but can be transferred to a GRAT. Instead of retaining the right to live in a residence for a term of years, as with a QPRT, the creator of a GRAT transfers the income-producing property to the GRAT and retains the right to receive a specific annual payment (the "annuity") for a term of years, after which ownership of the GRAT property passes to the designated GRAT beneficiaries. The value of the taxpayer's initial taxable gift is the value of the property contributed less the value of his or her right to receive the annuity payments for the term of years.

The value of the annuity payments is calculated at the creation of the GRAT using specific interest rate assumptions provided by the IRS each month, known as the applicable federal rate. A GRAT can be effectively structured so the taxpayer's retained annuity interest is exactly equal to the value of the property contributed, resulting in a taxable gift to the GRAT of zero.

Sales for a Self-Cancelling Installment Note (SCIN) or Private Annuity

Where a taxpayer desires to transfer property but needs to secure his own financial well-being from the property, a self-cancelling installment note (SCIN), private annuity, or straight installment sale may be appropriate. We cover installment sales in Chapter 6. SCINs and private annuities are both techniques designed to freeze the gift and estate tax value of appreciating property to the value at the date of a sale. A SCIN is essentially a self-cancelling installment note, which provides that future payment obligations cease at the earlier to occur of the expiration of a specified period or a specified contingency (generally the seller's death).

With a SCIN, the taxpayer sells real estate to children or other family members and finances the purchase with an installment note. Under a SCIN, the buyer will never pay more than the negotiated amount and may pay less. Because the buyer may pay less (if the seller dies before the note is paid in full), the buyer is required to pay a premium either in the form of a higher interest rate or more principal. The goal is for any remaining unpaid note amount not to be included in the taxpayer's estate at his death. With a sale for a private annuity, the taxpayer transfers real estate to children or other family members and reserves the right to receive a fixed annuity amount each year until his death. The amount of the annuity is determined by the taxpayer's actuarial life expectancy and the applicable federal interest rate in the month of transfer.

You do not incur gift-tax liability with a properly executed sale for a SCIN or private annuity, and the value of the property transferred will be excluded from your taxable estate upon death.

Special Valuation Rules for Farming or Business Property

The Internal Revenue Code allows real estate used for farming or in a trade or business to be valued (for purposes of calculating the federal estate tax) on the basis of its actual use rather than its fair market value if a series of complex requirements are satisfied. Farming is broadly defined. Trade or business other than farming is not defined but does not include passive rental or other passive investment activity.

The tax code may also allow a qualifying estate to pay the estate taxes attributable to a decedent's closely held business over an extended period of time. The maximum deferral allows the first payment to be made on the fifth anniversary of the original due date for payment of the tax and the balance to be paid in ten annual installments with interest. Only interest must be paid during the initial five-year period. The interest rate is normally 2 percent and may not apply to all the tax owed. There are several technical requirements, so talk with your tax advisor if you think you could use this strategy.

Charitable Strategies

When most of us think of making a charitable gift, the first method that comes to mind is to pull out our checkbook. Cash gifts, however, are donations of after-tax money and provide only limited tax benefits. Gifts of appreciated real estate, on the other hand, can provide greater value to the charity and save you income and/or estate taxes like few other gifts. In addition, these gifts can enable investors holding appreciated real estate to diversify their real estate holdings and create cash flow.

There are many charitable planning techniques available using real estate—ranging from simple to complex. Regardless of complexity, charitable gifts of real estate should be planned with your tax advisor and attorney. Some of the most effective charitable strategies using appreciated real estate are outright gifts to charity, bargain sales, gifts of undivided interests, gifts of remainder interests, charitable remainder trusts, charitable lead trusts, and qualified conservation contributions.

Outright Gifts of Real Estate

So long as a donor is not considered a dealer (someone who holds property primarily for sale to customers in the ordinary course of his trade or business, see Chapter 1), he can generally deduct the fair market value of a property transferred outright and irrevocably to charity, determined as of the date of contribution. In most cases, income tax is not imposed upon the charitable transfer or upon a subsequent sale of the real estate by the charity. Because the transfer is to a charity, it is not subject to gift tax, and the donor's taxable estate is reduced by the fair market value of the property.

Ordinarily, the income tax charitable deduction is limited to 30 percent of a donor's adjusted gross income for the year of the gift, and any excess unused deduction may be carried over for up to five years. This percentage limitation can be increased to 50 percent under certain circumstances.

Bargain Sale to Charity

Another option is to sell real estate to a charity for less than fair market value (known as a bargain sale). The donor will be entitled to an income tax deduction for the difference between the sale price and the fair market value and have taxable gain only to the extent the sales price exceeds the adjusted basis.

Gifts of Undivided Interests

A donor can gift an undivided portion of her entire interest in a property to charity. If a donor only owns a partial interest in a particular piece of real estate, she can gift all or part of that interest to charity. For example, a donor who owns a 70 percent interest in a piece of real estate can make a gift of 50 percent of her interest to charity. To qualify for a charitable deduction, such a gift must be carefully drafted to transfer a fraction or percentage of each and every substantial interest or right the donor owns in the property and must extend over the entire term of the donor's interest.

Gift of a Remainder Interest in a Personal Residence or Farm

A donor can also create a current income tax deduction by gifting a personal residence to a charity but retaining a life estate. This can be a particularly attractive option because it allows the donor to occupy and enjoy the property during his or her lifetime while also generating an immediate income tax charitable deduction.

Charitable Remainder Trust

Highly appreciated nonresidential real estate not subject to a mortgage can be an ideal asset to fund a charitable remainder trust (CRT). Highly appreciated nonresidential property can be contributed to a CRT tax free. The donor retains the right to receive annual income payments from the CRT in exchange for eventually passing the trust assets to the charity. The donor can also receive an income tax deduction for the present value of the charitable remainder interest that will pass to the charities.

Charitable Lead Trust

A charitable lead trust (CLT) is sometimes called a reverse CRT because it simply reverses the parties receiving the income and remainder interests. Specifically, the charity receives the income interest, and the assets remaining in the CLT and at the end of the term pass to the donor's heirs either free of gift or estate tax or at a substantially reduced rate.

Qualified Conservation Contributions

An outright contribution by a donor of his or her entire interest, a remainder interest, or an easement interest in real estate to a qualified organization for conservation purposes entitles the donor to a current charitable deduction. For example, a rancher may donate a portion of his land to a local land trust to be held as a wildlife corridor. The donation will entitle the rancher to claim an income tax deduction based on the decrease of the value of his ranch as a result of the conservation easement.

Common Pitfalls of Charitable Real Estate Donations

Because the potential tax savings available to charitable donors who make gifts of real estate can be so significant, the federal government has created a complex set of rules that donors and charities must follow. Failure to comply with one or more of these rules can lead to major tax problems. The most common traps involve valuation and substantiation issues, gifts of mortgaged property, prearranged sales, self-dealing prohibitions, and unrelated business income tax. Talk to your tax advisor and lawyer for more information about these common traps and how to avoid them.

CLOSING NOTES

For many people, real estate is the most significant component of their estates. It is also the asset that people hope to pass on to their loved ones with a minimum of hassle, taxes, and confusion. Using appropriate family and charitable planning strategies, owners or appreciated real estate can significantly decrease transfer and income tax and leave a legacy of smart planning. Here are a few final notes to close this chapter.

➤ Real estate titled in joint tenancy between a deceased person and a surviving joint tenant will pass to the surviving joint tenant—regardless of what the deceased joint tenant intended or provided in his or her will or revocable trust.

➤ Estate taxes will apply if the value of a deceased person's assets passing to nonspouse and noncharitable beneficiaries exceeds the applicable exclusion amount ($2 million for 2008), regardless of whether those assets pass via will, revocable trust, or joint tenancy.

➤ In 2008, you can gift up to $12,000 (this amount will likely change in coming years) to any number of individuals and an additional $1 million over your lifetime without incurring gift taxes.

➤ Use a qualified personal residence trust (QPRT) or a grantor retained annuity trust (GRAT) to freeze the value of real property for estate tax purposes while retaining the right to use it or receive income with qualifying properties.

➤ Use a self-cancelling installment note or private annuity to transfer real property to family members and reduce the size of your taxable estate while retaining the right to receive payments from the property.

➤ The estate of a deceased family member that owns real property used for farming or in a trade or business or that owns an interest in a closely held business may be eligible for special valuation rules that could reduce estate taxes and/or allow payment of estate taxes to be deferred.

➤ Gift appreciated property to a charity and receive an income tax deduction and avoid taxable gain on the untaxed appreciation. The charity can generally then sell the real estate tax free.

➤ Sell appreciated property to a charity for less than fair market value (known as a bargain sale) and receive an income tax deduction for the difference between the sale price and the fair market value and have taxable gain only to the extent the sales price exceeds your adjusted basis.

CHAPTER 12

Start a Family Limited Partnership

You hear a lot of dialogue on the death of the American
family. Families aren't dying. They're merging into big
conglomerates. A man should never neglect his family for
business.

—Erma Bombeck

Real estate investing, like farming or other small businesses, is
often a family affair. What starts off as one investment property can grow into multiple holdings that require regular management. Even if your children or other family members are not going
to immediately be active in the business, shifting some of the value of
these assets to them during your lifetime can make sense for your family
and your tax bill. One way to do this and still maintain control over your
assets is through a family limited partnership (FLP). FLPs present some
challenges, but when done right they can protect your assets from creditors and accomplish a number of estate planning and business goals.

THE ABCS OF FAMILY LIMITED PARTNERSHIPS

An FLP is not a unique entity; it is simply a limited partnership or limited liability limited partnership like those explained in Chapter 10,
except that the partners are normally family members. Typically you
and your spouse are the general partners, and your children or grandchildren are the limited partners. The general partners manage the business

PERSONAL SERVICES OF GENERAL PARTNERS

If all the income of the FLP is attributable to the personal efforts of the donor partner (likely a parent), then the donor will be taxed on the entire income. Capital of the partnership must be a material income-producing factor to validly split or shift income to all the partners. If capital is not a material income-producing factor, then it will mostly likely be considered an invalid attempt to assign income.

of the FLP, so you retain control of the partnership assets. The children start out as, and many times remain, limited partners. Limited partners do not participate in the day-to-day management of the FLP.

Income from the FLP is distributed to all of the partners according to their partnership interests (on a pro-rata basis). This can reduce income taxes by shifting income to the children who may be in a lower income tax bracket. However, the child must be recognized as a partner for income tax purposes for this to work. A partner is one who owns a capital interest in a partnership in which capital is a material income-producing factor.

Capital can be just about any real property, personal property, or intangible property that can produce income. Real estate can clearly be income-producing capital for a partnership, which makes it a good asset for an FLP.

In addition to distributions, the general partners can pay themselves a reasonable salary for managing the property held by the FLP. This enables the parent general partners to be compensated for their efforts even after they have transferred most of their interests and therefore receive very little from any distributions. In fact, they must receive reasonable compensation when they perform services for the FLP.

When the FLP is originally formed, a husband and wife will oftentimes contribute property or other capital to the partnership in exchange for their interests. The transfer of property or other capital to the FLP in exchange for the partnership interests is normally not a taxable event.

The husband and wife begin by owning both the general partner and limited partner interests. Then they begin making transfers of limited partnership interests to the children through a gifting program that utilizes the annual gift-tax exclusion amount ($12,000 per person per recipient in 2008) or their lifetime gift exclusion amount

($1 million during the donor's lifetime). If both parents utilize their annual gift-tax exclusion amount, they can transfer $24,000 per year (for 2008) to a single recipient. This can decrease the value of the parent's estate for estate tax purposes.

In addition, by placing assets in an FLP and then transferring partnership interests to the children (instead of transferring an interest in the capital itself), the annual gift-tax exclusion can be leveraged. Since limited partners have limited management rights, and limited partnership interests have no real marketability (that is, they could not easily be sold), the gifts of partnership interests may be discounted.

Advantages

When properly formed and maintained, an FLP can allow you to efficiently manage a family business enterprise, provide for family succession and estate planning, maintain control of the partnership capital, accelerate gifting to other family members, potentially reduce income and estate taxes, protect your assets, and maintain privacy. Chapter 10 provides many of the details about partnership management, asset protection, and conduit tax treatment (that is, avoiding double taxation), so we will not repeat those topics here. Following are some of the other advantages as they apply to FLPs.

Keep Control

Despite the potential income and estate tax advantages of making lifetime transfers or gifts, many people fear losing control of the property they would transfer or gift and do not take advantage of this as early as they could. The FLP eliminates this fear by having two types of ownership interests: general partners with management rights and limited partners without management rights. You can retain control of the management and operations of the partnership despite owning only a small general partnership interest. Or if you prefer

> **IT IS BEST TO CONTRIBUTE UNENCUMBERED PROPERTY**
>
> When encumbered property is transferred, it is important to determine the tax basis of the property before making a contribution. If the amount of the encumbrance exceeds the tax basis, an income tax may be due. The argument is that the contributing partner receives phantom income by being relieved of the obligation to pay the encumbrance to the extent it exceeds his tax basis.

to give management rights to a child, you can transfer a general partnership interest to him or her. This can be very helpful if a general partner becomes unable to manage the affairs of the partnership. Plus, this can normally be done without court involvement. Without the partnership it is possible that the courts would have to formally appoint a child or someone else to manage the property. Even better, if you are shifting control to your children, you could have them contribute working capital (personal services) in exchange for their interests.

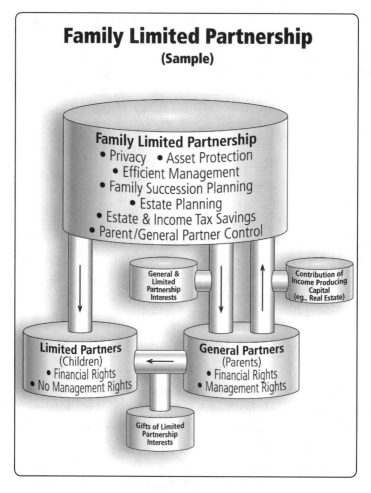

FIGURE 12.1 Family limited partnership

Family Succession and Estate Planning

The FLP can provide for continuity even upon your death; the partnership agreement can list successor general partners, allowing you to incorporate your succession plan into the partnership agreement in the event of incapacity. Finally, general partners may have more room to make aggressive business judgments because they are typically held to a lower standard of care (although there is still a standard of care!) than many other fiduciary relationships. (For example, a trustee of a trust is subject to the higher standards of a prudent investor.)

Leverage Gifting

Another advantage, as we introduced earlier in this chapter, is the leveraging effect that is created by gifting partnership interests rather than the underlying capital.

Example: You transfer income-producing property worth $100,000 to an FLP in exchange for both general and limited partnership interests. You then want to gift limited partnership interests to your two children using the annual gift tax limits of $12,000. The partnership agreement has strict limitations on transfers of partnership interests, and no management rights attach to the limited partnership interests. The value of the gifted limited partnership interests is discounted because of these restrictions on transferability and lack of management rights. This discount, if based on accurate appraisals, can enable you to transfer more than $12,000 in value of the underlying capital to each child. If you had transferred a fractional interest in the actual property, you would be limited to a fractional interest in the property worth $12,000. Plus, transferring a fractional interest directly, without an FLP or some other type of entity, can create other issues such as management agreement and succession problems.

Even with the benefits of leveraging, reducing the size of your estate may be a challenge with rapidly appreciating property. The value of a partnership interest gift is established on the date of the gift. If a general partner retains a large partnership interest, the increasing value of the partnership property will increase the value of the general partner's estate, which may make an annual gifting program less effective. There are other strategies that can be used in conjunction with an FLP,

> **CHILDREN'S LIMITED PARTNER INTERESTS**
>
> Consider using trusts to hold the children's limited partner interests. You could receive even more asset protection if the children's limited partnership interests are held by spendthrift trusts instead of outright.

including an installment sale or a grantor retained annuity trust (GRAT), which we discussed in Chapter 11, that can be used to transfer future appreciation out of your estate.

Avoid Probate and Maintain Privacy

Holding assets in an FLP keeps family business private during lifetime and after death. Property held in an FLP does not need to go through the public probate process. In addition to maintaining privacy, avoiding probate can save your heirs time, money, and aggravation. If you own property in more than one state, this is really important since you are required to go through probate in any state in which you own property.

Protect Assets

The protection offered by an FLP is twofold. First, the liability of a partner is limited to his investment in the partnership. This protection applies to acts of the partnership but will not insulate you from personal guarantees or personal liability for negligence or other torts. Second, in most states a creditor's remedies against a limited partner are restricted to a charging order (see Chapter 10). A charging order only allows the creditor to become an assignee of the limited partnership interest, and as an assignee the creditor's rights are limited to distributions declared by the general partners. The creditor has no power to force the FLP to make distributions (unless there is a bad partnership agreement or all of the other partners consent). This is a significant deterrent to most creditors, and they would rather settle than wait for a distribution or litigate to penetrate the FLP and force foreclosure.

As with the other asset protection strategies discussed in this book, remember that diversification is the key to maximizing the effectiveness of a given strategy. Transferring all of your assets to an FLP or any other single entity is probably not a good idea. Consult with your tax and legal advisors to determine an appropriate mix of strategies for your circumstances. Do not forget to update your plans and strategies as your circumstances change.

Rules of Operation

All of these advantages do not come easy. You must follow certain rules and procedures to have your FLP recognized as a partnership for state and federal tax purposes. Following are a few of the most important rules and procedures that apply in most cases. The exact rules and procedures will depend on your circumstances. FLPs should not be used without the advice of a competent tax advisor and lawyer.

> **REAL ESTATE AND FLPS**
>
> It is best to keep homes and vacation homes out of FLPs. Draft examples in the Treasury regulations suggest that there can be no substantial business purpose for contributing a vacation home to a partnership. While these examples were withdrawn from the final regulations, a significant district court case supported the idea that personal-use properties, such as homes or vacation homes, should not be included in a partnership because they may not satisfy the applicable rules.

Substantial Business Purpose

The partnership must have a purpose other than tax avoidance, and the FLP cannot simply be a shell created for the purpose of holding an asset until you can transfer it to limited partners. The IRS may recharacterize an entity for tax purposes if it does not have a substantial business purpose. It is critical to specifically and clearly state nontax objectives in the partnership agreement. It can also help to wait some time after the entity is formed before gifting partnership interests to your children. A critical distinction to remember is that an FLP is a business entity, not a family trust.

Contribution of Capital

Capital must be contributed to the FLP in order for a person who receives a partnership interest to be treated as a partner for federal income tax purposes, and the capital must be a material income-producing factor with respect to the FLP's business. If most of the FLP's income is generated from the personal services of the general partners (for example, fees and commissions earned by the parents) rather than from the capital of the partnership, then the limited partners will not be recognized as true partners unless they too contribute personal services. This is why real estate is a great asset to contribute.

Extreme care must be taken in preparing the partnership agreement to comply with state and federal tax law. If protection from creditors is a concern, then the agreement should contain provisions that inhibit the ability of creditors to reach the assets of the partnership. Proper documentation should also be prepared to convey assets to the FLP and to assign partnership interests to limited partners. And the FLP should have periodic partnership meetings to make decisions and conduct business, provide periodic reports to the limited partners, file an annual partnership tax return, and perform other functions consistent with running a true business.

Rights of General and Limited Partners

Another area that requires careful attention is structuring and maintaining the proper relationship between the general and limited partners. In one famous case, the tax court agreed with the IRS that the partnership's assets should be brought back into the decedent's estate because he retained control over the beneficial enjoyment of the assets. As the general partner, the decedent could determine when and in what amounts distributions were made and together with the other partners could terminate the partnership at any time and distribute its assets to the partners. A balance must be struck between giving the general partner the control he desires and restricting that power enough to keep the partnership from being disregarded for tax purposes.

While the general partners have all of the management rights, a limited partner must receive his partnership interest free of impermissible strings. If you transfer a limited partnership interest to a child and retain too much control, the limited partner may not be recognized as a true partner for tax purposes. An example of retained control that might create a problem is the right to decide who receives income rather than basing it on actual interests held in the partnership.

Recognition of partnership income, as we have stated before, must be allocated pro rata according to partnership interests. Some general partners are tempted to shift the larger portion of the income to children who are in a lower tax bracket. However, doing so will subject you to additional scrutiny and possible disqualification by the IRS. The same applies to depreciation and other tax items. A 50 percent limited partner should receive 50 percent of the depreciation rather than having the depreciation specially allocated to the general partner.

PARTNERSHIP TERMINATION WARNING

Transferring more than 50 percent of the total partnership interests in the FLP within a twelve-month period will terminate the partnership.

At the other end of the spectrum, the general partners must be compensated fairly for their management services. Either taking no compensation or taking too much compensation can subject the FLP to challenge by the IRS. For example, if the FLP owns a shopping center and a general partner is managing the shopping center yet takes no income, then the partnership income that was intended to be assigned to children would likely be taxable to the general partner who performed the management services. What is considered fair compensation can be a wide-ranging dollar amount. Consider not only what the actual services are worth but other compelling issues, such as specific expertise.

Minors' Interests in FLPs

Minors and other legally incompetent persons are allowed to own interests in FLPs. These interests can be held by a custodian under certain state laws, or by a trustee under a trust account. The state laws in this area vary greatly. Extra care should be taken when the person who donates a limited partnership interest to the minor also acts as the custodian or sole trustee for the benefit of a minor. This may cause the minor's interest to be includable in the donor's estate and may raise questions about whether the donor is acting solely in the interests of the minor.

One benefit of using FLP interests for gifts to minors that are held in custodial accounts is that it solves the problem of relinquishing control of the assets to the minor when she reaches legal adulthood. If you transfer cash to a custodial account, once your child reaches the age of eighteen (in most states), she would have full control over the cash—not the best planning strategy, even with precocious eighteen-year-olds. However, if the asset is a limited partnership interest, the child's rights are controlled by the partnership agreement, which can restrict transfer and use of the assets.

PLANNING FOR DISCOUNTS

One of the primary goals of discount planning is to reduce estate taxes by shrinking the size of your taxable estate. As discussed in Chapter 11, the estate tax law is currently in flux, and there is no consensus about whether it will impact more or fewer people in coming years. Even though many commentators feel that fewer people will need to plan for estate taxes in the future, discount planning with FLPs will likely always provide an estate planning technique for individuals with large estates. Two types of discounts may be available when valuing a limited partnership interest: lack of marketability and lack of control.

Lack of Marketability

Marketability refers to how quickly and cost-effectively an investor can convert an investment into cash. A discount for lack of marketability is an amount or percentage deducted from the value of an ownership interest based on its reduced marketability. Because most FLP agreements restrict the partners' rights to sell or transfer their partnership interests, a limited partnership interest can have reduced marketability. A prudent investor would not pay the same price for an outright interest in a property as a limited partnership interest in an entity that holds title to the property where she has little opportunity to resell her interest.

Lack of Control

A discount for lack of control is an amount or percentage deducted from the value of a partnership's interest to reflect the absence of some or all of the rights to control or manage the affairs of the partnership. Limited partners usually do not have any right to participate in the day-to-day business of the partnership. They usually have very limited rights to compel distributions or liquidation. In addition, because the partnership income is attributed directly to the partners regardless of whether the income was distributed, limited partners may have phantom income without the corresponding cash to pay the tax bill. Most investors would find this possibility undesirable.

How to Calculate Discounts

We are not going to tell you how to calculate discounts. Sorry. This is a very sensitive area and experts are constantly grappling with this issue. The discount you take should be determined by you and your advisors.

As you might imagine, people have taken discounting to the extreme, and, naturally, the IRS has started paying close attention to how discounts are applied and calculated. You will stand a much better chance of having a discount pass muster with the IRS if you use a qualified appraiser who specializes in this field.

In fact, 2007 was arguably a tough year for FLP valuations. Two high-profile federal cases were decided against taxpayers forming faulty FLPs. In both cases the taxpayers made major mistakes, including FLPs formed with no legitimate nontax purpose, FLPs paying for deceased taxpayer's personal bills, and deathbed transfers of assets into FLPs that left the taxpayer impoverished. A well-organized and properly operated FLP used for legitimate purposes, following the suggestions in this chapter, would avoid those mistakes.

While we will not provide specific suggested discounts, we will explain ways to use discounts. The discounts for lack of control or marketability are not mutually exclusive. If they both apply to an interest, then they can be combined. In addition, these discounts can apply to both general and limited partners. The fact that you transfer property from your name outright to an FLP potentially creates a discount for you even if you retain the bulk of both the general and limited partnership interests.

Again, do not try this yourself; hire an expert who will give you a full report on the valuation and heed this expert's advice. An initial appraisal will need to be completed as of the date you transfer assets into the FLP. If you are making annual gifts of your partnership interest, you will need to update the appraisals annually. While the cost of having regular appraisals done can be high, the cost of not doing them can be even higher. If the IRS challenges a discount, the appraiser's report can serve as your best defense.

LLC INSTEAD OF FLP

Practitioners sometimes use limited liability companies to accomplish the same goals as FLPs. This is not surprising because limited liability companies and FLPs can look and act substantially similar. If they are so similar, why might someone use an LLC instead of an FLP? It really depends on state laws relating to LLCs and FLPs. For example, in certain states, an LLC may offer greater liability protection. This may be true in states that do not have limited liability partnership laws.

In some states there may be significant disadvantages to using an LLC. For example, if state law gives a member the right to withdraw from the LLC and receive the fair market value of his or her interest, this freedom of transferability can reduce the size of discounts available for LLC interests. It may be possible to include language in the operating agreement to cover any disadvantageous default rules. A competent lawyer should know which entity will work best to accomplish your goals.

CLOSING NOTES

FLPs are not suitable for everyone, especially those who cannot or do not want to abide by the restrictions necessary to operate and properly maintain the partnership for tax purposes. That said, when done properly, FLPs offer many advantages.

➤ Provide efficient management and succession planning for a family business.
➤ Allow parents to maintain control of the partnership assets.
➤ Save income taxes by assigning income to family members in lower income tax brackets.
➤ Efficiently reduce possible estate taxes by leveraging gifts of partnership interests and reduce the size of your estate through discount planning.
➤ Avoid probate and maintain privacy.
➤ Protect assets from creditors.

The key to properly structuring an FLP is to follow these guidelines with approval of experienced legal counsel.

➤ Make sure the FLP has a substantial business purpose and treat it like a business, not a family trust.

➤ Draft a partnership agreement that complies with federal and state tax law and carefully defines the role of the general and limited partners.

➤ Contribute income-producing capital to the FLP.

➤ Devise an annual gifting plan for partnership interests that takes advantage of the annual and lifetime gift-tax exclusion amounts.

➤ Document every significant action of the FLP.

➤ Do not take a discount without having a qualified appraiser do the math.

CHAPTER 13

Leave Heirs a Stepped-Up Basis

*The only difference between death and taxes is that death
doesn't get worse every time Congress meets.*

—Will Rogers

The concept of a stepped-up basis has been part of our tax code for about eighty years. The general idea is that when a property is inherited its tax basis is stepped up to the fair market value at the time of the original owner's death. This adjusts the value of the property for inflation and can dramatically decrease the tax due if the new owner sells the property for more than its stepped-up basis. The new owner only pays tax on the increase in value while she owns the property. Stepped-up basis is discussed primarily in the context of estate planning, but in order to be fully utilized it must be understood when acquiring property and deciding how it should be held. In this chapter, we explain stepped-up basis as it relates to real property and discuss the best strategies for maximizing your use of this wealth-preserving strategy.

WHAT IS A STEPPED-UP BASIS?

Before we delve into stepped-up basis, a quick review of basis is in order. Basis is important to real property owners since it has a significant impact in determining taxable profit or loss when a property is sold. In Chapter 1, we discussed how to calculate the basis and how it may adjust during ownership. Remember that adjusted basis is the original or cost basis (purchase price) plus capital additions (qualifying improvements) plus the cost of sale minus depreciation. If the property has appreciated

NO TRANSFERS IN CONTEMPLATION OF DEATH

It may be tempting to transfer property to a dying parent or spouse in order to benefit from a full stepped-up basis, but it is not advisable. The stepped-up basis rules do not apply to appreciated property you receive from a decedent if you or your spouse originally gave the property to the decedent within one year before the decedent's death. Your basis will be the same as the decedent's adjusted basis in the property immediately before his death rather than the fair market value.

in value since its acquisition, it is highly likely that the basis is less than the fair market value of the property. When the property is sold, you pay capital gains taxes on the difference between the sales price and your adjusted basis. For example, if you sold the property for $400,000 and your adjusted basis was $150,000, then your taxable profit would be $250,000.

Simple math tells us that decreasing the spread between the sales price and the adjusted basis lowers the tax bill. Stepped-up basis does just that by increasing the basis of inherited property to, in most cases, the fair market value of the property at the time of the decedent's death. If the property's fair market value at the time of death is $400,000 and the new owner sells it for $400,000, then no federal income tax will be owed. Note that stepped-up basis applies only to federal income tax, not to inheritance or estate taxes.

As you can imagine, receiving a stepped-up basis for highly appreciated assets that have been held for a long period of time is very beneficial to heirs.

The stepped-up basis rules apply to property acquired by bequest, devise, or inheritance, so it does not matter whether the decedent has a will or dies intestate (without a will). The general rule states that your basis in property inherited from a decedent is the fair market value of the property at the date of the decedent's death. There is an alternative valuation method that allows you to elect to value the property six months after the date of death or at the date of disposition, if earlier. This alternative is primarily used for estates that have experienced a decline in the value of assets during the six-month period. There are also special rules for valuing property used in farming or a closely held business or that is a qualified conservation easement.

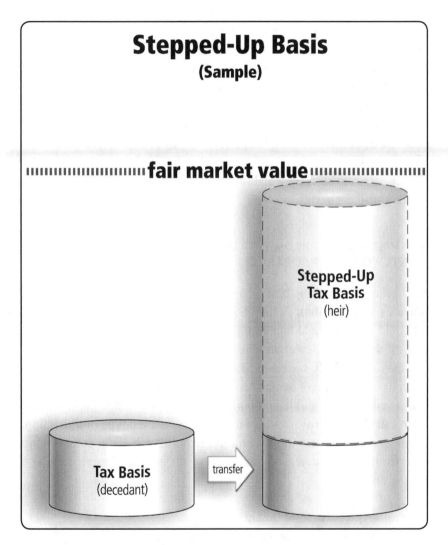

FIGURE 13.1 Stepped-up basis

The bad news for high-net-worth taxpayers is that the unlimited stepped-up basis is set to expire for decedents dying after December 31, 2009 and is replaced with a limited stepped-up basis for qualifying estates. After 2009, qualified estates are limited to $1.3 million of stepped-up basis for nonspouse heirs. Spouses can receive an additional $3 million. This change is tied to the same act that will make the estate tax go away for at least one year and then snap back to its pre-act status after 2010 unless a future Congress elects to continue the legislation. We have yet to meet someone who can predict what Congress will do on this matter (or any other matter); therefore, it is still advisable to plan for a step-up in basis, even if limited.

In most cases it is best to plan for tomorrow, at least where taxes are concerned. Consistent with that policy, we assume the current unlimited basis rule applies in the remainder of this chapter. It remains important to keep accurate basis information for all of your assets so that your heirs can determine a basis.

MAXIMIZING STEPPED-UP BASIS WITH JOINTLY OWNED PROPERTY

As simple as stepped-up basis sounds, some planning is required to maximize its full potential. A full step-up in basis is available for property inherited from a single owner, but what happens if a property is jointly owned? Most spouses choose to jointly own their primary residence and may also jointly own a vacation home. The answer to this question depends on the form of ownership (joint tenancy or tenancy in common) and whether a community property regime applies since there are different survivorship rules and tax implications to each type of ownership. Legal forms of ownership and the particular rules about survivorship vary from state to state, so consult with your attorney before making a final decision.

Property Held in Joint Tenancy

Joint tenancy is one of the most common forms of ownership of real property, especially for spouses. It is a type of ownership by two or more persons (not legal entities) in which each owns an undivided interest in the whole and has a right of survivorship. The right of survivorship is the distinguishing feature of joint tenancy. Upon the death of a joint tenant, the entire ownership automatically vests in the surviving joint tenant or in equal shares if there is more than one surviving tenant. Because this transfer occurs automatically, property held in joint tenancy does not require probate (the legal process for administering someone's estate).

Joint tenancy is thought to be an equitable form of ownership that protects each tenant's individual rights in the property. Each joint tenant is legally entitled to the right of possession and cannot be excluded by the other joint tenant(s). Depending on state law, each tenant may have a right to a pro-rata share of any income from the property regardless of his contribution to the purchase price. In most cases, joint tenants are free to sell or encumber their portion of the property without the consent of the other joint tenants.

In joint tenancy, only the decedent's interest in the property receives a step-up in basis. For example, suppose a husband and wife hold, as joint tenants, property with a basis of $200,000. The husband dies and the property is appraised with a fair market value of $300,000. The basis for the deceased husband's share of the property is adjusted upward from $100,000 to $150,000. Adding that to the wife's existing basis of $100,000 brings her total adjusted basis for the property to $250,000. This significantly reduces the potential tax liability on a sale, but it does not come as close to eliminating it as would a full step-up in basis.

Property Held in Tenancy in Common

When you do not specify joint tenancy in the vesting deed to the property, the default form of ownership that applies in most states is tenancy in common. One significant way tenancy in common differs from joint tenancy is that it does not provide a right of survivorship. This means that when a co-owner dies her interest does not automatically pass to the other co-owners. She can bequeath her interest to a new owner of her choosing in a will.

The ownership in a tenancy in common is based on a stated fractional interest that usually relates to the portion of the purchase price supplied by each owner. Two individuals, even if they are married, could own a property as tenants in common with one owner owning 70 percent and the other owner owning 30 percent. In contrast, in a joint tenancy with right of survivorship where a husband and wife are the joint tenants, one-half of the value of the property is included in the deceased spouse's estate regardless of how much each spouse contributes to the purchase price.

The heir of a tenancy-in-common interest gets a step-up in basis for the fractional share of the property inherited from the decedent. In this sense, a tenancy in common is similar to a joint tenancy. Married couples tend to be more comfortable with the right of survivorship offered by joint tenancy. Tenancy in common is a popular way to hold title for a group of real estate investors because it allows the owners to leave their individual share of the investment to whomever they designate according to their will instead of to the other co-owners. Before deciding to use this form of ownership you need to consider how to protect yourself from a co-owner's creditors, how to manage the property, and what happens upon death of a co-owner or sale of a co-owner's interest.

PRESERVING COMMUNITY PROPERTY

Married couples owning community property generally receive a full step-up at the death of the first spouse. When one spouse dies, both halves of the community property receive a step-up in basis, unlike with property held jointly or as tenants in common, in which case only the decedent's one-half interest in the property receives a step-up. Obviously, community property offers a huge tax advantage as long as the stepped-up basis rules still apply.

So how do you get community property? You must reside in and acquire property in a state with a community property regime. The general theory of community property is that all property acquired during marriage, with the exception of that acquired by gift, devise, or descent, is owned equally by the spouses. States currently having community property systems accepted by the IRS are Arizona, California, Idaho, Louisiana, Nevada, New Mexico, Texas, Washington, and Wisconsin. Some of these states require you to recite in the deed that the property will be held as community property. States without a community property system are known as common law states.

Given the large stepped-up basis benefit at stake, care must be taken when titling and transferring community property to avoid destroying the community nature of the property. There are several issues that must be carefully researched depending on the state of residence and the location of the property. Following are a few questions that highlight some of the typical issues that arise:

➤ Can a property located in a community property state qualify as community property if the owners title the property as a joint tenancy?

➤ Can the property qualify as community property if it is transferred to a revocable trust?

➤ What happens when a married couple moves to a common law state and retains property located in a community property state where they used to reside?

➤ What happens when a married couple resides in a common law state and acquires property (such as a vacation property) in a community property state?

Generally, the law of the state where real property is located controls the characterization of the property. However, not all states follow this general rule, and each state differs on how actions such as divorce or death impact community property. Many common law states provide a mechanism for maintaining the status of property as community property. Colorado, for example, has a law that preserves the community property character of a property for purposes of disposition on death.

Colorado also has a law that provides that real property is not presumed to be community property where the property is located in Colorado and titled as joint tenants with rights of survivorship even though the married persons acquired the Colorado property with community property. This presumption can be rebutted if the couple can show they intend to preserve the community property character of the joint property. An example of intent would be a recitation in a deed stating that the spouses intend for the property to retain its community property character.

Preserving community property can be complex and requires the assistance of a knowledgeable attorney. Unfortunately, many people mistakenly believe estate planning has become less important because current estate tax laws have significantly reduced the number of individuals who are subject to the estate tax. However, the estate tax is only one reason to complete an estate plan. The top priorities include family harmony and security. Another important priority is to reduce or eliminate nonestate taxes, including capital gains taxes, by properly titling capital assets and preserving community property.

ESTABLISHING THE STEPPED-UP BASIS

As discussed earlier, a stepped-up basis is based on the fair market value of the property as of the date of death or six months after. The safest method of establishing fair market value is to use a qualified appraiser. You could gather data yourself by asking for comparables from a real estate agent; however, appraisers are usually worth the cost because the thorough documentation provided by a qualified independent appraiser is your best defense if the valuation is challenged by the IRS. Valuations can differ among appraisers, and it may be worth your while to shop around for an appraiser you feel will provide the most accurate appraisal for your circumstances.

The IRS defines fair market value as "the price the property would sell for on the open market." It is the price that would be agreed upon between a willing buyer and a willing seller, meaning that the parties are not required to act and both parties have reasonable knowledge of the relevant facts. If you have just inherited the property and are selling it on the open market immediately, the actual sales price in an arm's-length transaction will almost always be considered the fair market value. The value is more difficult to establish for properties that have been held for some time after inheritance without filing for a stepped-up basis. Fortunately, most appraisers can give you an appraisal of the property at any particular point in time, within a reasonable historical period.

Professional real estate appraisers traditionally use three basic valuation techniques to estimate the fair market value of a property:

1. *Sales comparison approach* (using market data). The sales comparison approach uses market data for similar properties to estimate the value of the subject property. The accuracy of the sales comparison approach is highly dependent on the market data for the recent sales of comparable properties. Typically, appraisers use the best three comparable properties in close proximity to the subject property. An

appraiser will then adjust up or down depending on the differences between the subject property and the comparables.

2. *Cost approach.* The cost approach to valuing real estate relies on the fact that an informed buyer would not pay more for a property than it would cost to build a comparable property. This approach is sometimes used where there is a lack of available data on comparable properties and for proposed construction or brand new properties. With this approach, the property is divided by improvements (build-ings) and land, and each segment is valued separately.

3. *Income capitalization approach.* This method is primarily used for larger income-producing properties. The approach is based on the principle that the higher the income, the more valuable the prop-erty. Capitalization is a process of converting an income stream to a value using a "cap rate," or capitalization rate. Good real estate agents often know current cap rates in the local market, and you can actually derive the cap rate yourself by examining recent sale prices for similar properties if you also have reliable information regard-ing their net operating income. The cap rate can be calculated using the following formula: R (capitalization rate) = NOI (net operating income) / V (value).

In order to minimize capital gains taxes through a stepped-up basis, it is generally to your advantage to establish the highest possible fair mar-ket value. However, it is not always the case that a high fair market value is the best strategy for your circumstances. There may be other factors that outweigh the capital gains savings. For example, business succession planning often requires balancing the interests of the various parties. An heir or partner who is buying out the interest of a deceased partner may want a more conservative valuation.

Plus, estate tax savings strategies could be more important than capi-tal gain tax savings strategies. If a deceased person's estate is or may be subject to estate taxes, a conservative valuation may make more financial sense. For estates of individuals dying after 2005, the maximum rate for the estate tax is 45 percent, while the current capital gains tax rate is 15 percent. Under these circumstances, it may be best to go with a lower fair market value (and lower stepped-up basis) to minimize current estate taxes. Whether someone is subject to estate taxes depends on whether the estate exceeds the applicable exclusion amount (the amount that an individual can pass estate tax free):

APPLICABLE EXCLUSION AMOUNTS	
Year	Exclusion Amount
2008	$2,000,000
2009	$3,500,000
2010	Repealed
2011	$1,000,000

Income taxes may also need to be weighed. A common method of reducing income taxes from income-producing property is to make a gift or other transfer of the property during one's lifetime (an inter vivos gift) to a donee in a lower income tax bracket. This can also transfer future appreciation to the donee and out of the donor's estate for estate tax purposes. However, in most cases, the donee of an inter vivos gift takes the donor's basis. Under these circumstances, the loss of the stepped-up basis must be weighed against the income tax and estate tax savings.

Clearly, some strategizing and financial planning is required before you hire an appraiser to determine the fair market value of the decedent's property. Talking with your financial advisors and estate planner can help you determine the best strategy. Once a fair market value is established, you must actually file for the stepped-up basis. Your tax advisor can help you with the details of actually filing.

CLOSING NOTES ON STEPPED-UP BASIS

Leaving real property to your heirs or inheriting real property is an excellent tax strategy because of the advantages of receiving a stepped-up basis. When a property is inherited, its tax basis is stepped-up to the fair market value at the time of the original owner's death or six months after death. This reduces or eliminates the amount of tax due when the new owner sells the property since the new owner does not have to pay tax on the gain accumulated during the decedent's lifetime. Here are a few more notes to remember from this chapter.

➤ Stepped-up basis is discussed primarily in the context of estate planning, but in order to be fully utilized it must be understood when acquiring property and deciding how it is to be held.

➤ If you co-own real property in joint tenancy or tenancy in common, the deceased owner's separate interest in the property will receive a step-up in basis.

➤ If you live in a community property state or own community property, be sure to take advantage of receiving a full step-up in basis.

➤ Proper estate planning can help you title property to avoid probate and determine whether maximizing a step-up in basis makes sense given potential estate taxes.

➤ Remember, you must take action to receive a step-up in basis, namely filing the appropriate forms with the IRS.

PART FIVE
Use Alternative Strategies

CHAPTER 14

Invest in Real Estate
with an IRA

*The most powerful force in the universe is compounding
interest.*

—Albert Einstein

Many people do not realize that they can use their IRA to invest in real estate. The same tax and compounding benefits you receive on the stocks and bonds owned by your IRA can also be received on real estate investments. By investing in real estate through an IRA, taxable gain and income can be deferred or even eliminated. In addition to the tax benefits, adding real estate to your retirement portfolio can provide diversification. Only truly self-directed IRAs allow direct real estate investment, but the number of IRA administrators who provide this option has grown significantly. That said, this is a complex area and is probably best suited to individuals who are experienced real estate investors. In this chapter, we introduce you to the basics of investing in real estate with an IRA.

OVERVIEW OF RETIREMENT PLANS

There are many types of retirement plans. We are not going to review each type in detail here since that would end up being a separate book. Our focus is on the plans that enable real estate investing and whether it makes sense for you.

Tax-Deferred and Tax-Free Plans

Retirement plans are generally either *defined benefit plans*, which promise a certain benefit at retirement, or *defined contribution plans*, which provide for current contributions to retirement accounts but do not guarantee the benefits paid at retirement. Most plans today are defined contribution plans. These plans can be further divided into those that are sponsored by employers and those adopted by individuals. Common employer-sponsored plans include profit sharing, 401(k), and pension plans. The most common individual plans are traditional and Roth individual retirement accounts, otherwise known as an IRA and a Roth IRA. All of these plans may be generically referred to as qualified retirement plans because they are approved by the IRS and established in the federal tax code to receive special tax treatment.

Very few employer-sponsored plans allow the participants to invest in real estate; however, the number of IRA administrators that allow real estate investments continues to grow. We focus on using an IRA in this chapter, but the concepts should also apply to employer-sponsored plans that permit real estate investments.

Most retirement accounts are tax-deferred plans. Contributions to the plan are deductible, so they reduce the taxpayer's gross income in the year the contribution is made. The tax-deferred characteristic of the plan refers to the fact that earnings on contributions made to the plans grow tax free until distributed. When you begin taking distributions at retirement, the distributions are subject to tax at your ordinary income tax rate. You must begin taking distributions from a traditional IRA after age seventy and a half, and the distribution amount must comply with the required minimum distribution rules.

On the other hand, Roth IRAs are tax-free retirement plans. Contributions to Roth IRAs are made with after-tax dollars, so there is no immediate tax advantage or deduction in the year the contribution is made. Like traditional IRAs, the earnings on contributions grow tax free. The difference and big advantage of a Roth IRA, however, is that distributions made from the Roth IRA are tax free as long as the taxpayer is over fifty-nine and a half years old and the distribution is made at least five years after the initial contribution. Another advantage is that distributions from a Roth IRA do not need to begin during the lifetime of the person who set up the plan, so you can delay distributions beyond age seventy and a half to maximize investment growth.

Many financial experts favor the Roth IRA. They say the ultimate return on a Roth IRA will exceed that of a traditional IRA under many circumstances. If you expect to buy a real estate investment with IRA funds and hold it for a long period, a Roth IRA is most likely your best option, particularly if the property appreciates significantly. Most people have tax-deferred plans and enjoy the yearly deductions provided by these plans, but if you are going to do a lot of real estate investing, it may be best to convert to a Roth IRA in the long run.

You can convert a traditional IRA to a Roth IRA as long as you meet certain earnings requirements and pay the applicable ordinary income tax on the conversion. Under current law, the income limitation to convert a traditional IRA to a Roth IRA will remain $100,000 of adjusted gross income until 2010. Beginning in 2010, as part of the Tax Increase Prevention and Reconciliation Act of 2005 (TIPRA), all taxpayers will have the option to convert their traditional IRA to a Roth IRA regardless of income level. (This assumes Congress will not change its mind.)

The challenge is that the assets converted from a traditional IRA to a Roth IRA are treated as ordinary income and recognized in the year of conversion. For a conversion occurring after 2009, however, a taxpayer will be permitted to spread the tax cost over two years. If you are under fifty-nine and a half years old and use assets from the converted traditional IRA to pay any taxes due on the conversion, you will incur a 10 percent penalty for early withdrawal.

While converting to a Roth IRA may seem attractive, there are a number of factors to consider in addition to the tax-free distribution benefit. The current tax costs may outweigh the future tax savings, for example, if the investment return is questionable. If you need to use a non-IRA source of funds to pay the taxes due on conversion, you will need to consider whether the earning potential of those funds in their existing investment is better than the advantages to be gained by conversion. Talk to your tax and financial advisor to determine whether converting a traditional IRA to a Roth IRA is best for you.

Self-Directed Accounts

Since 1975, individuals rather than their employers have been able to choose where their retirement funds are invested within the limits of the retirement plan. Today, standard investment choices include mutual funds, stocks, bonds, and certificates of deposit. Real estate is a nonstandard asset, but it is not a prohibited investment. The IRS only prohibits two types of investments: life insurance contracts and collectibles. Whether you can invest in real estate with a particular retirement account depends on the custodian or trustee in charge of the plan and the investment provisions written in the plan documents.

Only a truly self-directed account allows you the freedom to buy and sell nonstandard investments, including real estate, at your discretion. Both IRAs and qualified plans can be self-directed. In most cases, employer-originated retirement plans will not enable you to invest in nonstandard assets like real estate, but you should check with your plan administrator. If your employer's plan does not allow for real estate investments, you may have to roll over your retirement funds from the employer's plan to your own self-directed IRA.

Of course, most IRAs are managed by large investment firms who may discourage (or prohibit) their customers from investing in nonstandard assets since they are more management intensive and may reduce fees. Some of the large investment firms offer pseudo self-directed IRAs that allow investors to choose from a number of preselected investment options. Many of these options are simply prepackaged stocks, bonds, and mutual funds that are marketed as self-directed.

When establishing your own self-directed IRA, you will need to locate a third-party administrator that specializes in real estate and work with that administrator to set up the account. It is important to select a knowledgeable administrator who has experience with the type of property you intend to purchase. Fees and terms can vary widely among administrators. Be sure to ask about the fees charged per real estate transaction.

You will also want to ask about the types of property permitted and the availability of services related to the property type. Most IRA custodians that hold real estate will allow you to purchase raw or vacant land, residential properties, or commercial buildings. Some custodians may even permit investments in foreign property, REITS, and real estate notes. If you intend to hold income-producing real property, you may want an administrator that provides the service of collecting rent or paying expenses.

Successful self-directed investing requires quite a bit of financial analysis and investment savvy and is best for those who have experience investing in real estate. Adequate insurance can protect some of the risk. Most banks provide insurance for deposits through the Federal Deposit Insurance Corporation (FDIC), which guarantees the protection of up to $100,000 of the uninvested cash in your account. Note that FDIC insurance only covers uninvested assets, not invested assets. Make sure the uninvested cash in your self-directed account is FDIC insured.

MANAGING REAL ESTATE IN A SELF-DIRECTED PLAN

Once you have established and funded your self-directed retirement account, the administrator should provide a procedure for investing in real estate. As a general matter, the mechanics of purchase and sale transactions are the same as if you were personally handling the transaction. The main difference when using IRA funds is that the plan trustee or administrator is technically purchasing or selling the property on behalf of your IRA. As a result, title to the property will be held in the name of the administrator for the benefit of your IRA.

All cash in and cash out related to the property must go through the IRA and comply with IRA distribution rules. If you put up earnest money with your personal funds, you will need to make sure the title company reimburses you out of escrow at closing and replaces it with funds from your IRA. If you purchase income-producing property, all of the income must be deposited in your IRA account. Similarly, all property expenses, including taxes, insurance, and repairs, must be paid from the funds in your IRA. This means that your IRA needs to have available cash. You can continue to make annual contributions to your IRA within federal contribution guidelines and may need to do so to cover expenses if the property does not generate enough income.

It is possible to sell the real estate held by your IRA by making a request to your administrator. Once the transaction is closed, all of the proceeds from the sale must stay in the IRA in order to maintain its tax-advantaged status. A possible alternative is to sell an IRA-held property with seller financing so that all payments made by the buyers are paid to the IRA and become tax-deferred income.

At this time, there is not a rule governing the percentage of IRA assets that can be in the form of real estate, so it is possible for the account to be entirely made up of real estate. However, real estate is an illiquid investment; if your IRA is going to hold real estate, then you need to plan for retirement with this in mind. Having too much of the account tied up in illiquid real estate will reduce the amount of funds available for distribution during retirement. As you approach retirement, the IRA may need to sell real estate or convert it to an income stream.

Self-Dealing and Prohibited Transactions

There are a few transactions that are prohibited by an IRA. It is important to understand these prohibited transactions, since engaging in one can terminate your IRA's tax-advantaged status. The key is that there can be no self-dealing with IRA funds, that is, taking advantage of the IRA to further personal objectives other than those permitted by the plan. Examples of prohibited transactions include:

➤ Selling property you own to an IRA.
➤ Borrowing money from your IRA.
➤ Receiving unreasonable compensation for managing assets owned by your IRA.
➤ Using your IRA as security for a loan.
➤ Buying property for present or future personal use with IRA funds.

The IRS will penalize improper use of your IRA by you, your beneficiary, or a disqualified person. A disqualified person in this context includes your fiduciary and your family members (a spouse, ancestor, lineal descendant, or spouse of a lineal descendant). It also includes any partnerships or entities in which you own a majority interest. A fiduciary is essentially anyone who exercises discretionary control or authority in managing or administering your IRA.

Engaging in a prohibited transaction may jeopardize the tax status of the IRA. The IRS may even treat the account as having distributed all of the assets at fair market value on the first day of the year in which the prohibited transaction took place, which can result in a large amount of taxable gain. There may also be an additional 10 percent tax penalty on early withdrawals. Fiduciaries who engage in a prohibited transaction may be charged a penalty tax of up to 100 percent of the amount involved if they do not correct the transaction during the taxable period.

Remember that the purpose of an IRA is to provide a retirement benefit, and its tax status hinges on this purpose. It is not meant to provide a present benefit to you or to a disqualified person. You cannot place real estate that you or a family member already own into your IRA since the IRA would be purchasing the property from you or the family member. Another example of receiving a present benefit is using the real estate owned by your IRA as your residence or vacation home or office. A less obvious example is having a construction company that you own develop a tract of land held by your IRA.

Notwithstanding the prohibited transaction rules regarding personal use, you can withdraw real estate from your IRA and use it as a residence or second home when you reach retirement age, which is fifty-nine and a half or older for penalty-free withdrawal. Any time after that point, you can elect to take an in-kind distribution of the property. Under the in-kind arrangement, your IRA custodian assigns the title to the property to you. You will then have to pay income taxes on the current value of the property if it has been held in a traditional IRA. If the property was held in a Roth IRA for over five years, you may not owe any tax at distribution. To spread the tax costs, you could transfer the property in a series of undivided interests over the years and you will only be taxed on the fair market value of the undivided interest, but you cannot live in the property until it has been completely distributed.

Borrowing Money

It is common for investors to use leverage to increase the investment return of a property and build real estate wealth. However, with IRAs this is a sensitive area and it is usually best to purchase real estate without a loan. Clearly, you cannot borrow money from your IRA to purchase a property since that would be self-dealing. If the IRA does not have sufficient funds to purchase the property without a loan, then the IRA may need to borrow money.

The loan must be transacted entirely between the IRA and a third-party lender. So you will need to find a lender willing to make a nonrecourse loan to the IRA or locate a property with seller financing. You cannot guarantee the loan or use your credit to secure the loan since doing so may be considered a prohibited transaction. The property should generate enough income for the administrator to make the loan payments or you will need to make an additional contribution to the IRA to cover the payments. Keep in mind that there are contribution limits that apply to IRAs. For 2008, individuals can make IRA contributions up to the lesser of $5,000 ($6,000 if age fifty or older) or 100 percent of the individual compensation.

The biggest problem with borrowing money arises from an IRS rule regarding unrelated business income tax (UBIT). This rule imposes a tax on tax-exempt organizations, including traditional and Roth IRAs, when they earn income from activities that are not substantially related to their exempt purpose. Rents from real property are excluded from the definition of unrelated business income, so purchasing rental property in an IRA is not by itself a problem. The problem arises when the rental property is leveraged.

IRS Publication 598 specifically states that income from debt-financed property is subject to UBIT. Debt-financed property is any property held to produce income for which there is acquisition indebtedness at any time during the tax year. Acquisition indebtedness is the outstanding amount of principal debt incurred by the IRA to acquire or improve the property:

➤ Before the property was acquired or improved, if the debt was incurred because of the acquisition or improvement of the property, or

➤ After the property was acquired or improved, if the debt was incurred because of the acquisition or improvement and the organization could reasonably foresee the need to incur the debt at the time the property was acquired or improved.

$1,000 EXEMPTION

There is a small allowance: if the net income on all debt-financed property is $1,000 or less in a twelve-month period, then UBIT will not apply.

The result of using debt financing is that income or gain that would otherwise be tax deferred or tax free in your IRA is taxed. If the IRA sells debt-financed property, you must include a percentage of any gain or loss when computing UBIT. The percentage is that of the highest acquisition indebtedness of the property during the twelve-month period preceding the date of sale in relation to the property's average adjusted basis.

The good news is that there are ways to decrease the amount of income subject to UBIT. An IRA can deduct certain operating expenses related to the property and take depreciation using the straight-line method. These deductions can be used to offset income. Another option may be to use excess income to make lump-sum principal reduction payments each year. Once the debt is paid off, the income from the investment is no longer subject to UBIT because the investment is no longer a debt-financed property.

Avoiding debt financing altogether may be possible since an IRA can acquire an undivided interest in real property. If a real estate investment opportunity exceeds the resources of your self-directed IRA, then it may be wise to partner with others in the investment. The partners do not necessarily need to provide other IRA funds. The IRA may even partner with you to acquire partial interests in the property as long as you comply with the rules regarding prohibited transactions.

CLOSING NOTES

Investing in real estate with an IRA may be a great way to diversify your retirement portfolio and manage real estate investments in a tax-free or tax-deferred environment. Gains are tax free in an IRA since nothing is taxed until distribution. And with a Roth IRA, even the distributions will be tax free. A self-directed account must be set up in order to invest in real estate. Below are key points to consider when investing in real estate with an IRA.

➤ IRA funds may be used to purchase real estate, including leveraged real estate, as long as the transaction is carefully structured and managed.

➤ When an IRA owns leveraged real estate it may incur unrelated business income without proper planning.

➤ All transactions should be arm's length and not directly involve the IRA owner or a member of his family.

➤ An IRA may purchase rental property or vacation property as long as it is not used by the IRA owner or a member of his family for personal use.

➤ When using IRA funds to invest in nonstandard assets like real estate, it is best to consult your tax advisor beforehand.

CHAPTER 15

Explore Foreign Real Estate

So I was now the owner of a villa whose lands it would take
two oxen two days to plow. Owning neither an ox nor a
plow, I'd have to take their word for that.

—Frances Mayes, *Under the Tuscan Sun*

Traveling abroad has long been a dream for many Americans. The memoir quoted above sparked another dream for many people: owning real estate abroad. Romantic notions aside, there are practical reasons for investing in foreign real estate. Some experts feel that foreign real estate markets will offer greater money-making opportunities than the U.S. market in the coming years. Despite its growing popularity, owning real estate in another country raises complicated legal and tax issues and often comes with a few surprises. In this chapter, we highlight key differences between U.S. real estate transactions and non-U.S. transactions. We also cover the basics of the income and estate tax consequences of foreign real estate investments.

WHY LOCALS ARE GOING GLOBAL

The motivation to seek out foreign real estate investments varies with the investor, but in most cases people are seeking pleasure, portfolio diversification, or profit.

The type of property purchased and financial strategy used depends on the motivation behind the purchase. Those motivated by pleasure may be looking for a vacation property in a location with certain perks: a warm place to spend the winter, a retreat for family and friends, or a diverse cultural experience. They may also be looking for an affordable place to retire. A retiree who has worked and owned a primary residence in the United States may have an easier time affording a luxury condominium in a place like Mexico, or Costa Rica. Retirement dollars may not go as far in the United States, particularly in highly appreciated markets like California.

Those motivated by portfolio diversification are less concerned with the perks of a given location and more with looking for a safe way to balance out other investments. The profit-motivated investor expects high returns and looks for opportunistic strategies unique to certain countries. Acting on these motivations can be a challenge, but it is becoming easier. For example, India eased restrictions on foreign real estate ownership in 2005, and some estimate the market values there to be appreciating at an annual rate of 30 percent.

How They Do It

Search for international real estate on the Internet and you will realize that finding a property abroad to purchase is not too difficult. The difficulty comes in dealing with unfamiliar foreign property and tax laws. To limit the number of unexpected issues that arise during and after the acquisition, it is best to assemble a team of real estate experts to assist with the transaction. The type of real estate expert you need will depend on the form of your investment. There are essentially three ways to invest in international real estate:

1. Direct property ownership.
2. Foreign REITS.
3. Mutual funds and exchange-traded funds.

Direct property ownership is a large category in itself and encompasses all kinds of ownership structures, from sole ownership to various forms of shared ownership like time-shares. When buying property abroad, you will likely need a U.S. attorney who can work with an attorney or notary where the property is located and a real estate agent or broker. Real estate brokers can be found in most countries. Be aware, however, that in some countries this profession is not regulated or licensed like it is in the United States. In addition, the services performed by brokers can differ greatly between countries. Take the time to find a reputable real estate agent or broker and be sure to ask for details about the services this person will perform.

If you are more motivated by portfolio diversification and profit than by the pleasure of owning a vacation home in a far away land, then you may be able to achieve that diversification through real estate investment trusts (REITS). REITS are privately held or publicly traded companies that own income-producing commercial real estate. In the United States, REITS are exempt from paying corporate income taxes, provided that the REIT receives a large majority of its income from real estate and annually distributes between 75–100 percent of its earnings to shareholders in the form of dividends. Foreign REITS may have similar rules. You may purchase shares of the REIT itself or find a mutual fund or exchange-traded fund (ETF) that includes REITS. An ETF is a security that tracks a specific index, commodity, or category of asset (like commercial real estate in Asia) and is traded like a stock. ETFs are normally more tax efficient and have lower operating and transaction costs than actively managed mutual funds.

Without REITS, only very wealthy individuals or institutional investors could afford to own international commercial real estate. REITS allow more investors to benefit from growth in this sector without having the capital and expertise required to own the property directly. Publicly traded REITS are also a more liquid investment than direct property ownership. Australia and the United States were pioneers in the market, and many more countries have passed legislation approving REITS in the last decade.

The risk and potential profit from a given REIT are tied to its sector and geography. For example, a REIT that specializes in shopping centers in Sydney will not perform well if that market slumps. A less risky way to invest in REITS is to diversify with a mutual fund or ETF. While REITS typically specialize and own real estate directly and may or may not be successful at it, a mutual fund or ETF is normally more diversified by owning a collection of publicly traded stocks. The fund manager actively trades and diversifies the fund to limit its volatility. A particular fund may hold publicly traded companies that own real estate or REIT.

Owning foreign real estate can offer true diversification to your investment portfolio since real estate is inherently geographic and tied to local economies. For example, the apartment market in London will be different than the apartment market in Tokyo since the economic conditions for apartments are different in each of those markets. In addition, owning foreign real estate offers currency exposure to your investments. While diversification does not ensure profit or prevent loss, it can reduce the volatility of returns over the long term.

What Are the Risks and Rules?

Some risks of owning real estate in foreign countries are unique, and some are the same as with U.S. real estate, but more exaggerated. Our focus is on the risks associated with the legal and tax regimes. A basic assumption of international law is that property is subject to the laws of the country in which the property is located. Because this assumption is true in most cases, it is possible that owning property in another country may conflict with or even invalidate U.S. financial or estate planning that involves a foreign property. It is also possible that you could buy a piece of property and find out later that you do not really own it—at least the way you thought you did. Foreign laws can affect the rights you have as a property owner in many ways, including those discussed in the following sections.

Eligibility

If you choose to own foreign real estate directly, believe it or not, the first question you must ask is whether you may own property in that country. Many countries prohibit real property ownership by foreign nationals. These prohibitions can be absolute or partial. A partial prohibition may restrict the geographic area in which foreigners can own property, or it may limit the type of ownership rights. For example, Switzerland strictly prohibits non-Swiss citizens from owning a main residence there and limits the purchase of a secondary residence by noncitizens to small parcels in authorized locations.

A desire to participate in free trade and the global economy has led many countries to enact land-reform legislation that encourages foreign investment. So it is often possible to legally avoid laws restricting ownership by applying for permits or acquiring the property through an appropriate legal structure. Be certain that these methods are acceptable to the relevant government authority. Also, be sure to determine the impact of any acquisition permits or restrictions on the resale or transfer of the property. Acquiring the property may be a short-term gain and long-term loss if you cannot sell it or transfer it to your heirs.

Form of Ownership

Even if foreign nationals and noncitizens are allowed to own property in a given country, there may be laws that restrict the form of ownership. These laws may dictate whether the property can be held in a trust, in a corporation, or in a person's name. Some countries require nonresidents to hold property in either a trust or corporate entity.

Aside from local laws that control the form of ownership by nonresidents, there are estate and tax considerations that need to be factored into the decision about whether to hold property directly or through some type of trust or entity. For example, in France any property that is owned directly is subject to forced heirship rules, but these rules can be legally avoided by holding the property in a special type of nontrading investment company.

If the property must be owned through a trust in order to comply with eligibility laws or to be consistent with estate planning objectives, then you must remember to include the cost of setting up the trust in your acquisition costs. Trusts can be expensive to create and maintain. Oftentimes, the trust administrator will charge annual administrative fees that can be fairly expensive. And paying a U.S. attorney to work with local counsel may also be expensive.

Transfer or Sale

There can be many kinds of restrictions on the sale or transfer of property. Some of these restrictions apply to resale and others to transfer upon death. Many countries have matrimonial property regimes and forced heirship laws that favor transferring real property to spouses and family members regardless of the decedent's stated intentions in a will. There also may be a legal pre-emption right or right of first refusal in favor of the local government, a neighbor, or a lessee or tenant. Historical buildings and agricultural land are particularly likely to come with a right of first refusal in favor of the local government or current tenants.

Finally, real property located in the United States and real property located outside the United States are not considered like-kind properties for the purpose of a tax-deferred like-kind exchange (see Chapter 7). So if you were planning to use a like-kind exchange to sell U.S. real property and buy foreign real property or vice versa, you will need to change your plans.

Control or Use

It is even possible that your use of the property may be restricted by local laws. There are many types of restrictions, but the most common are easements or servitudes. Easements or servitudes require the property owner to tolerate certain intrusions or restrict the ability of the property owner to use the property in a certain way. Restrictions on the use of property to protect the environment, agricultural lands, and historical and cultural buildings are common in many countries. Some restrictions date back to feudal times. For example, some properties still have encumbrances that obligate the property owner to perform certain actions, such as supplying a certain amount of wheat to the local government. Another example is restrictions that require using historically authentic building materials when making repairs or improvements to a structure. It may be possible to release these restrictions by paying a fee.

Liability

Real property in any location can be the source of liability from third-party claims. How local laws compensate for and remedy this liability can vary greatly. Some countries have lower thresholds for civil litigation than others. What happens if a contractor is injured replacing a roof on your Swiss chalet? What if the neighbor's prize greyhound falls into the well of your English country home? If the property is rented, what are the tenant's rights?

There are many ways to protect your assets from seizure and liability, but the method used depends on the legal regime where the property is located and whether it is possible to devise a legal structure to avoid the application of default laws. It is best if these issues are researched and handled before the property is purchased. And it is imperative to have your U.S. attorney work with local counsel in the country where the property is located.

TAXES

Once the property rights issues are clarified, the next step is to understand the tax impacts of owning foreign real property. Real property is usually taxed by the government where the real estate is located, but the asset value, income, and gain may be taxed by both the local government and the government where the property owner is domiciled. There are three sources of tax laws for U.S. citizens who own foreign real property:

1. The laws of the United States.
2. The laws of the country where the property is located.
3. International treaties.

Using available treaties and applicable exemptions or deductions can make it possible to avoid being taxed twice for the same transaction, income, and gain. Finding an applicable treaty or double-taxation agreement between the interested countries is the key to avoiding double taxation.

Though many people may think owning property abroad is a tax shelter, most developed countries have tax laws that discourage people from investing all their money in foreign countries with lower tax rates. And while reducing or avoiding taxes is an acceptable goal of international investing, evading taxes is another issue and one that will get you into trouble. It is always best to be transparent, especially since there are plenty of ways to achieve tax savings through legitimate means.

Besides, the laws require transparency. The United States imposes special tax rules and reporting requirements on U.S. citizens who own foreign assets through non-U.S. entities or trusts. And the same tax treaties and agreements that save you from double taxation often include an exchange-of-information clause that requires the countries to share information about taxpayers.

EXPATRIATES

Do not think that you can avoid federal taxes by becoming an expatriate. The United States has tax authority over certain former U.S. citizens for ten years after expatriation.

Purchase and Transfer Taxes

Most countries charge a tax when real property is transferred from one owner to another. These transfer taxes can be 5 percent or more of the purchase price, depending on the country. Newly built property may be subject to a sales tax or value added tax (VAT) instead of a transfer tax. VAT rates in the European countries can be around 20 percent. Notary and registry fees are often charged in addition to taxes, and it is best to get an estimate before closing, since these fees can vary greatly.

In some countries, simply transferring a property from your name to a corporation held by you may trigger the transfer tax. For example, Mexico imposes significant taxes on transfers of real property made during the owner's lifetime. This tax is broadly applied to any transaction where the property is deemed to trade hands. Be sure to check with a local lawyer before implementing business or estate plans that require changing title so that you do not inadvertently trigger transfer taxes.

Income and Wealth Taxes

It should be no surprise that most countries require payment of a tax on any capital gain resulting from the sale of real estate. Each country has a different tax structure for gain, and the rate may depend on whether the property is held directly or through a company. As in the United States, keep receipts and invoices for expenses and improvements since they may be deductable when calculating taxable gain.

Most countries also charge income tax on any revenue generated from renting real property. Simply owning property in another country may make you a resident of that country for income tax purposes. Some countries even charge income tax on imputed rental value. If you do not rent the property, the taxing authority will determine how much income could be obtained if it were rented and tax you based on this fictitious income.

Finally, a few countries charge general wealth taxes on the value of real estate. For example, Spain charges an annual wealth tax of 2.5

percent on large assets. There may also be annual charges, sometimes called stamp duty, for things like document administration, sewage connections, and garbage removal.

Estate and Gift Taxes

The gross estate of a U.S. citizen includes all property wherever situated, which means all real estate whether located in the United States or in a foreign country. Since the country where the property is located may also have a right to tax the property and its transfer, owning foreign real estate may be a real burden to an estate. As with the other tax areas previously discussed, there is often an applicable tax treaty or agreement that helps to reduce or eliminate this double tax burden.

Good planning and understanding of treaties is critical since estate taxes can be very high. There are a few countries that do not charge inheritance or estate taxes (for example, Italy), but most do. Some countries charge higher inheritance taxes based on the degree of relationship and wealth of the inheritor. For example, in Spain the highest inheritance tax rate for wealthy unrelated persons is 81.6 percent.

Changing Domicile

The discussion of taxes so far has assumed that the foreign real property owner was a U.S. citizen domiciled in the United States. The tax and planning issues get more convoluted when that assumption changes. Simply acquiring real estate in a foreign country does not make you a citizen of that country; however, domicile can be changed by default if you purchase foreign real property and spend a significant amount of time at the property. Of course, you may choose to change your domicile. For some individuals, changing domicile is the only way to reduce their tax burden.

Spending a few weeks a year at a vacation home in another country is usually not significant enough to raise tax residence issues. If you plan to spend several months each year out of the country, then you will need to consider the tax consequences. Many countries have the right to tax your worldwide income if you spend six months each year at your property in their country. Decide whether you intend to fully relocate to the new country or simply vacation there, and obtain legal guidance on domicile issues.

CLOSING NOTES ON OWNING FOREIGN REAL ESTATE

When considering a purchase of foreign real estate you must thoroughly research property rights, holding structures, and tax and estate issues before making a purchase. Assumptions about owning real property that are based on experiences in the United States do not necessarily apply to another country. Despite globalization, real estate remains inherently local; it is governed by local laws and subject to local economics. This is true whether you are buying a vacation home or are an international land developer. Also, remember that foreign real estate and U.S. real estate are not considered like-kind property and therefore cannot be exchanged tax free. Below are a few key questions to begin your research process.

1. What is my motivation or goal in purchasing real property in another country?
2. Can I and should I own the property directly, or must I or should I own it through a trust or company?
3. Can I own the property indefinitely or can I only own it for a term of years?
4. Can a title search be done to determine who has rights to the property, and if so, how certain can I be that I will own the property free and clear?
5. Can I rent or lease the property, and if so, who has the right to the income produced from the property?
6. Are there any pre-emptive rights or restrictions on the transfer or sale of the property?
7. What is my cumulative tax liability associated with the property, from acquisition to ownership to sale?
8. Can the property transfer to my benefactor of choice when I die or will local laws decide who gets the property?
9. What happens if there is an accident on the property or the property is destroyed by a fire, hurricane, or other disaster?
10. How much time do I plan to spend at the foreign property?

APPENDIX A

Online Real Estate Investment Strategies

"The Internet used to be nothing. Now it's everything. In 1995, you had to go see a real estate agent to look at homes and you couldn't get that listing book out of their hands. Now, you can go online to look up most houses for sale in the whole country. The volume of data available now is stupendous."

—*Steve Sawyer*

Today, the Internet plays a prominent role in the buying and selling of real estate and is an almost limitless source of real estate information. The tax and legal strategies described in this book will be used best if you first make well-informed buying and selling decisions. This appendix provides a roadmap of how most real estate is bought and sold today and supplies you with Internet strategies to empower your real estate investing decisions.

THEN AND NOW

Ten years ago, a search for real estate would have started in the office of a local real estate agent or by just driving around town. At the agent's office, you would spend an afternoon flipping through pages of active property listings from the local Multiple Listing Service (MLS). After choosing properties of interest, you would spend many weeks touring each property until you found the right one. Finding market data to enable you to assess the asking price would take more time and a lot more driving, and you still might not be able to find all of the information you needed to get really comfortable with a fair market value.

Today, most property searches start on the Internet. A quick search on *www.google.com* by location will likely get you thousands of results. If you spot a property of interest, you can typically view photos online and maybe even take a virtual tour. You can then check other websites, such as the local county assessor, to get an idea of the property's value; see what the current owner paid for the property; check the real estate taxes; get census data and school information; and even check out what shops are within walking distance—all without leaving your house!

While the resources on the Internet are convenient and helpful, using them properly can be a challenge because of the volume of information and the difficulty in verifying its accuracy. At the time of writing, a search of "Denver real estate" returned 2,670,000 websites. Even a neighborhood-specific search for real estate can easily return thousands of websites. With so many resources online, how does an investor effectively use them without getting bogged down or winding up with incomplete or bad information? Believe it or not, understanding how the business of real estate works offline makes it easier to understand online real estate strategies.

THE BUSINESS OF REAL ESTATE

Real estate is typically bought and sold either through a licensed real estate agent or directly by the owner. The vast majority is bought and sold through real estate brokers. (We use "agent" and "broker" to refer to the same professional.) This is due to their real estate knowledge and experience and, at least historically, their exclusive access to a database of active properties for sale. Access to this database of property listings provides the most efficient way to search for properties.

The MLS (and CIE)

The database of residential, land, and smaller income-producing properties (including some commercial properties) is commonly referred to as a multiple listing service (MLS). In most cases, only properties listed by member real estate agents can be added to an MLS. The primary purposes of an MLS include:

➤ A system to correlate and disseminate property listing information so real estate agents can facilitate the sale, lease, and exchange of their client's properties;

➤ A means by which member agents made offers of compensation to other member agents; and

➤ A means by which information is accumulated and disseminated to enable the preparation of appraisals, analyses, and other valuations of real estate.

These purposes did not include enabling the direct publishing of the MLS information to the public; times change. Today, most MLS information is directly accessible to the public over the Internet in many different forms.

Commercial property listings are also displayed online, but aggregated commercial property information is more elusive. Larger MLSs often operate a commercial information exchange (CIE). A CIE is similar to an MLS but the agents adding the listings to the database are not required to offer any specific type of compensation to the other members. Compensation is negotiated outside the CIE.

In most cases, for-sale-by-owner properties cannot be directly added to an MLS and CIE, which are typically maintained by REALTOR® associations. The lack of a managed centralized database can make these properties more difficult to locate. Traditionally, these properties are found by driving around or looking for ads in the local newspaper's real estate listings. A more efficient way to locate for-sale-by-owner properties is to search for a for-sale-by-owner website in the geographic area.

MLS and CIE property listing information was historically only available in hardcopy, and as we mentioned, only directly

WHAT IS A REALTOR®?

Sometimes the terms real estate agent and REALTOR® are used interchangeably; however, they are not the same. A REALTOR® is a licensed real estate agent who is also a member of the NATIONAL ASSOCIATION OF REALTORS®.

available to real estate agent members of an MLS or CIE. About ten years ago, this valuable property information started to trickle out to the Internet. This trickle is now a flood!

One reason is that most of the 1 million or so REALTORS® have websites, and most of those websites have varying amounts of the local MLS or CIE property information displayed on them. Another reason is that there are many non-real estate agent websites that also offer real estate information, including for-sale-by-owner sites, foreclosure sites, regional and international listing sites, county assessor sites, and valuation and market information sites. The flood of real estate information to the Internet definitely makes the information more accessible but also more confusing and subject to misunderstanding and misuse.

Real Estate Agents

Despite the flood of real estate information on the Internet, most properties are still sold directly through real estate agents listing properties in the local MLS or CIE. However, those property listings do not stay local anymore. By its nature, the Internet is a global marketplace and local MLS and CIE listings are normally disseminated for display on many different websites. For example, many go to the NATIONAL ASSOCIATION OF REALTORS® website, *www.realtor.com*, and to the local real estate agent's website. In addition, the listing may be displayed on the website of a local newspaper. In essence, the Internet is just another form of marketing offered by today's real estate agent, but it has a much broader reach than the old print advertising.

In addition to Internet marketing, listing agents may also help the seller establish a price, hold open houses, keep the seller informed of interested buyers and offers, negotiate the contract, and help with closing. When an agent provides all of these services, it is referred to as being a full service listing arrangement. While full service listing arrangements are the most common type of listing arrangement, they are not the only option anymore.

Changes in the technology behind the real estate business have caused many agents to change the way they do business. In large part, this is due to the instant access most consumers now have to property listings and other real estate information. In addition, the Internet and other technologies have automated much of the marketing and initial searching process for real estate. For example, consumers can view properties online and make inquires via e-mail. Brokers can use automated programs to send listings to consumers that match their property criteria. So, some agents now limit the services they offer and change their fees accordingly. An agent may offer to advertise the property in the MLS but only provide limited additional services. In the future, some real estate agents may offer services in more of an à la carte fashion.

Because of the volume of real estate information on the Internet, when people hire a real estate agent today they should look at the particular services offered by the agent and the depth of their experience and knowledge in the relevant property sector. It is no longer just about access to property listing information. Buyers and sellers historically found agents by referrals from friends and family. The Internet now provides ways to directly find qualified agents or to research the biography of a referral agent. Several sites offer searchable databases about real estate agents.

Some have argued that the Internet makes REALTORS® and the MLS less relevant. We believe this will be false in the long run. It may change the role of the agent but will make knowledgeable, qualified, and professional REALTORS® more relevant than ever. In fact, the number of real estate agents has risen significantly in recent years. No wonder; the Internet has made local real estate a global business. Besides, Internet or not, the simple fact remains that the purchase of real property is the largest single purchase most people make in their life (or, for many investors, the largest multiple purchases over a lifetime), and they want expert help. As for the MLS, it remains the most reliable source of real estate listing and sold information available and continues to enable efficient marketing of properties. So, what is the function of all the online real estate information?

Online real estate information is a great research tool for buyers and sellers and a marketing tool for sellers. When used properly, buyers can save time by quickly researching properties and, ultimately, make better investment decisions. Sellers can efficiently research the market and make informed decisions about hiring an agent and marketing their properties online. The next step is to know where to look online for some of the best resources.

INTERNET STRATEGIES

In the sections that follow, we provide strategies and tips on how to use the Internet to locate properties for sale and research information relevant to your decision to purchase the property. There are many real estate websites from which to choose, and although we do not mean to endorse any particular website, we have found the ones listed here to be good resources in most cases or to be so popular that they need mention. One way to test a website's accuracy is to search for information about a property you already own.

Finding Real Estate for Sale

Despite the widely available access to real estate listings, many believe that MLS databases continue to offer the most complete and accurate source of real estate information. Most MLSs now distribute content to other websites (primarily operated by real estate agents). An excellent starting point for MLS-originated content is the national MLS website, *www.realtor.com*, which is also the most popular website for searching real estate listings. Virtually all local and regional MLSs have an agreement with *www.realtor.com* to display much of their active listing inventory.

Some local and regional MLS systems also have a publicly accessible website with limited information. Ultimately, to get complete information, you will need to find a qualified local REALTOR®. Many local real estate agents will also provide their customers (via e-mail) new listings that are input into the system that match their predefined criteria. This can be very helpful to a busy buyer.

There are also many websites that display both real estate agent listed and for-sale-by-owner properties. Some of the more popular websites include *www.zillow.com* and *www.trulia.com*. These sites offer other services, too. For example, zillow.com is best known for its instantaneous property valuation function, and trulia.com is best known for providing historical information. Other sources of properties for sale are the state, regional, and local websites associated with brokerage companies; for example, *www.remax.com* or *www.prudential.com*. Search engines like *www.yahoo.com* and classified advertising sites like *www.craigslist.org* also have real estate listings.

One key difference between these sites is how much information you can access anonymously. For example, at *www.trulia.com* you can shop anonymously up to a point but then you will need to click through to the agent's website for more information. Many new real estate search engines allow you to sift through listings without having to fill out a form. The best strategy is to browse a few of the sites just listed to find geographic areas or price ranges that are interesting. Once you get serious about a property, that is the time to find a qualified REALTOR® of your choice to conduct a search in the local MLS.

It also never hurts to search the old-fashioned way by driving through the neighborhoods that interest you. There is no substitute for physically, not virtually, walking the block when you are making a serious investment decision. In this sense, real estate is still a very local business and standing in front of the property can lead to a much different decision than viewing a webpage printout.

Valuing Real Estate

As we mentioned, one of the most popular real estate tools is zillow.com's instant property valuation. Just type in an address and you get a property value. It even charts the price ups and downs, and shows the last date sold (including price) and the property taxes. There are other sites that provide similar tools such as *www.housevalues.com* and *www.homegain.com*. Unfortunately, many people use these estimated values alone to justify sales prices, offers, and counteroffers. However, these are only rough estimates based on a formula that incorporates the local county sales information. These estimates can swing wildly over a short period of time and do not appear to track actual market changes, which are normally more gradual. In addition, these estimates may not take into account property remodels or renovations or other property-specific or local changes. This is not to say these sites are not useful. In fact, they are great starting points and can provide a good ballpark value in many cases.

When it comes to getting a more accurate value for a particular property, there are other strategies that are more trustworthy. One is to go directly to your county's website. More often than not, the county assessor's area of the website provides sales and tax information for all properties in the county. If you want to research a particular property or compare sales prices of comparable properties, the local assessor's sites are really helpful. When you visit a county's website, you are getting information straight from the source. Most counties today publish property information on their websites. Many times you cannot only see the price a previous owner paid, but the assessed value, property taxes, and maps. Some county assessors are now adding market and property valuation tools, too.

Given the importance of valuation to investing, we are also going to remind you of the two most important (non-Internet) valuation methods: real estate agents and appraisers. Working with a local REALTOR® is an accurate and efficient way to get value information for a property. While one of the primary purposes of the MLS is to market the active property listings of its members, the system also collects sales information for those listings. REALTOR® members can pull this sales information and produce comparable market analyses (sometimes called CMAs) that provide an excellent snapshot of a particular property's value for the market in a particular area.

Finally, the most accurate way to value a property is by having a certified appraiser produce an appraisal. An appraiser will typically review both the sold information in the MLS system as well as county information and then analyze the information to produce a valuation for the property based on one or more approved methods of valuation. These methods of valuation can include a comparison of similar properties adjusted for differences between the properties, determine the cost to replace the property, or, with an income-producing property, determine a value based on the income generated from the property.

The Neighborhood

There are many ways the Internet can help you get the scoop on a particular neighborhood. For example, census data can be found at *www .census.gov.* You can also check out the neighborhood scoop at sites like *www.outside.in* or review local blogs. A blog is a website where people discuss topics by posting and responding to messages. Start by looking at *www.placeblogger.com* and *www.kcnn.org/citymediasites.com* for a directory of blogs. Trulia.com has a "Heat Map" that shows how hot or cold each neighborhood is based on prices, sales, or popularity among the site's users.

Schools

When it comes to selling residential property or rental properties that cater to families, the quality of the area's school district makes a huge difference. There are many websites devoted to school information. Check out *www.greatschools.net* or *www.schoolmatters.com*. Most local school districts also have their own websites. These sites contain a variety of information about the public schools and the school district, including its district demographics, test scores, and parent reviews.

Finding Real Estate Agents

A recent addition to the Internet boom in real estate information is the creation of websites that let real estate agents display their property listings and provide personal profiles such as their professional biographies. You can search to find an agent with particular expertise, geographic areas of specialization, and services offered. On some sites, these profiles will also include their featured property listings. For example, OpenHouse.com lists open-house information from all agents and brokers who want to join the site.

Maps and Other Tools

The Internet has made mapping and locating properties much easier. To get an aerial view or satellite image of a property or neighborhood, go to *www.maps.live.com* or *www.maps.google.com*, or visit *www .walkscore.com* to see how walkable a particular property is. These sites can give you an idea of the neighborhood characteristics and the types of entertainment, restaurants, and other facilities that are within walking distance of the property. Maps.Live.com provides a view at an angle so you can see the sides of houses, and Maps.Google even gives you a 360-degree street-level view for certain neighborhoods. If you have not tried one of these satellite map websites, you really should, if only for amusement's sake.

FINAL THOUGHTS ON INTERNET STRATEGIES

The Internet is a very effective research and marketing tool for real estate investors, but it is not a replacement for a knowledgeable and experienced real estate professional. The Internet can save you time and money by enabling quick and easy property research and marketing options. It can also help you efficiently find a REALTOR® who fits your buying or selling needs.

Always remember, when it comes to Internet strategies for real estate, more knowledge is better. You need to use the Internet to build your knowledge base on a target property or to find a real estate agent with expertise you need. However, the big caution here is that the Internet should *not* replace human judgment and perspective, expert advice, or physical due diligence—keys to successful investing.

APPENDIX B

Glossary

accelerated depreciation:
A method of calculating depreciation where deductions are higher in the early years of the asset's life, as compared to straight-line depreciation where deductions are equal for each year of the life of the asset. Accelerated depreciation can result in application of the alternative minimum tax.

accommodator:
See *qualified intermediary*.

accumulated depreciation:
The total depreciation taken on an asset since it was acquired.

active income:
Income from an activity in which you materially participate, for example, wages, salaries, and earnings from a business in which you materially participate. The distinction between active and passive income is critical because passive losses can only be taken against passive income, not active income. See also *material participation*.

active participation:
Involvement in a rental real estate activity making significant management decisions and using independent judgment.

adjusted basis:
An amount that is used to compute gain or loss on the disposition of property and to compute depreciation. As a general rule, the adjusted basis is the acquisition cost of an asset plus the cost of any capital improvements less depreciation.

adjusted gross income (AGI):
The amount of income that is taxable; gross income from all taxable sources minus all allowable adjustments.

alternative minimum tax (AMT):
An alternative tax system aimed at those with high incomes who would pay no income tax under the regular tax system because of certain deductions, exemptions, or other preferences. If the AMT calculation produces a higher tax liability than the regular calculation, then the taxpayer must pay the higher amount. The AMT catches a lot of real estate investors because a year with a large capital gain can trigger the AMT.

applicable exclusion:
An amount any one individual can pass to another without incurring estate taxes.

appraisal:
A professional opinion or estimate of the value of a property. The appraised value is the most likely price a seller would receive in an arm's-length transaction for the appraised property. Appraisals are usually performed using one or more of the following three methods: (1) cost of replacement, (2) value as a function of income produced by property, and (3) market comparison with similar properties.

appreciation:
An increase in the value of a property that can result from inflation, demand pressures, or improvements and modernizations made to the property.

articles of incorporation:
A document filed in most states with the secretary of state by the founders of a corporation specifying such items as the name, location, nature of the business, and capital investment. The document is also known as a certificate of incorporation. The corporation only comes into existence when the filing is approved by the state.

articles of organization:
Similar to articles of incorporation, but it is a document filed with the secretary of state by the founders of a limited liability company (LLC). It is also known as articles of formation.

at-risk rules:
Tax laws that limit the amount of loss an investor can deduct.

attorney-in-fact:
One who is authorized to act for another under a general or limited power of attorney.

balloon payment:
The final payment on a loan; this payment is greater than the preceding installment payments and pays off the loan.

basis:
The starting point from which gains, losses, and depreciation deductions are computed. Generally it is the acquisition cost or purchase price of an asset. See also adjusted basis.

beneficiary:
A person entitled to the benefits of a trust, will, insurance policy, or pension plan.

boot:
Money or non-like-kind property that is received as consideration in connection with a like-kind exchange.

buyer in a like-kind exchange:
The person acquiring the relinquished property in a like-kind exchange.

capital asset:
An asset that will be held over a long period of time and is not bought or sold in the regular course of business. Examples include land, buildings, and machinery.

capital gain:
An increase in the value of a capital asset that is not recognized until the asset is sold at a price that is higher than the purchase price.

capitalization rate:
The rate of interest used to discount the future income from a property to arrive at a present value.

capital loss:
A decrease in the value of a capital asset that is not recognized until the asset is sold at a price that is lower than the purchase price.

charitable remainder trust:
A trust in which the donor transfers ownership of an asset to a properly structured tax-exempt trust. The donor retains the right to receive annual income payments from the trust, and at the end of the term (usually the life of the donor and his or her spouse) the assets owned by the trust pass to one or more designated charities.

charitable lead trust:
Similar to a charitable remainder trust except that the charity receives the annual income payments, and the assets remaining in the trust at the end of the term can pass to the donor's heirs either free of gift and estate tax or at a substantially reduced rate.

closely held business:
A company with a small group of controlling shareholders.

constructive receipt:
A federal income tax concept that treats an exchanger in a like-kind exchange as receiving property or cash even though such payment has not legally transferred to the exchanger. This can happen when the exchanger has unrestricted use of the property or cash. A qualified intermediary can be used in these transactions to avoid constructive receipt.

Crummey trust:
A type of irrevocable life insurance trust that allows for tax-free gifts to minors by limiting withdrawals of interest or principal to a specified period of time. This type of trust does not require distribution of assets at age twenty-one like other trusts for minors.

dealer:
An individual or legal entity that invests to sell and is involved on a regular basis in the development, improvement, and advertisement of real estate for sale. The amount of taxes paid and planning options available often depend on the distinction between being an investor and a dealer in real estate.

deduction:
Any allowable item or expenditure that can be subtracted from gross income in order to reduce the amount of income that is subject to taxation.

deed:
A written document that conveys legal title to real property. Common types of deeds include a general warranty deed, quit claim deed, and special warranty deed.

deed of trust:
A security interest used in many states in lieu of a mortgage. The deed of trust is recorded with the county clerk and recorder of the appropriate county as public evidence of the lender's security interest in the property.

deferred exchange, or deferred gain:
A gain that is realized but not recognized as taxable income until a later time.

depreciation:
A decrease in a property's value over the time it is being used. This term can refer to an annual tax deduction for wear and tear and a loss of utility in a property. You can recover the cost of certain property by taking annual deductions for depreciation.

depreciation recapture:
Tax rules that require you to include all or part of the depreciation deducted in previous years in the current year's taxable income. When you sell depreciable property, you may be required to report as income all or part of the gain that is attributable to depreciation.

durable power of attorney:
A legal document that enables an individual to designate another person, called the attorney-in-fact, to act on his or her behalf in the event the individual becomes disabled or incapacitated.

equity:
The value of real property if you were to sell it, minus any debts you owe on it.

estate tax:
The amount of tax levied on a deceased individual's taxable estate; it generally consists of the value of the gross estate above a set exemption amount minus any allowable deductions.

exchange accommodation titleholder (EAT):
An individual or legal entity engaged by the exchanger in a reverse exchange to hold title to replacement property or, in rare cases, relinquished property to facilitate a parking transaction.

exchange agreement:
A contract entered into between an exchanger and a qualified intermediary providing, among other things, that the qualified intermediary will facilitate the exchange and hold the exchange proceeds subject to applicable restrictions.

exchange period:
The period beginning the day after the transfer of the relinquished property and ending 180 days later. This period will be cut short if the exchanger files the tax return for the taxable year of the exchange prior to the 180th day.

exchange proceeds:
Consideration received for the relinquished property.

exchanger:
An individual or entity pursuing a like-kind exchange.

exemption:
A deduction, based on a status or circumstance, allowed by law to reduce the total amount of taxable income.

fair market value (FMV):
The price at which a property would change hands between a seller and a buyer, neither having to sell or buy, and both having reasonable knowledge of all relevant facts.

family limited partnership (FLP):
A form of partnership where a family's assets are pooled into one family-owned partnership in which each partner owns an interest. Shares can be gifted to family members to take advantage of the annual gift-tax exclusion.

fee simple:
Standing alone, these words create an absolute estate in the person to whom property is given. These words may be followed by a condition or special limitation on the estate.

financing:
Rolling the costs of getting your loan (originator fees, closing costs, and so on) into the total loan balance in order to pay these extra costs along with your loan repayment.

fixture:
A thing that has been so permanently attached to real property that it is regarded as part of the real property. An example is a furnace affixed to a house.

grantor retained annuity trust (GRAT), or grantor retained income trust (GRIT):
A type of irrevocable lifetime trust in which the creator of the trust transfers income-producing property to the trust and retains the right to receive the income for a term of years, after which ownership of the trust property passes to the designated beneficiaries.

identification period:
The period the IRS gives an exchanger to identify in writing a replacement property to qualify for a like-kind exchange. This period begins the day after the transfer of the relinquished property and ends forty-five days later.

installment sale:
A sale in which the buyer pays the purchase price through a series of payments that are spread out over a period of time.

Internal Revenue Code of 1986, as amended (IRC):
This is the main body of United States statutory tax law and is published at Title 26 of the United States Code.

investor:
An individual or legal entity that invests to hold and is interested in the appreciation and cash flow from real property. The amount of taxes paid and planning options available often depend on the distinction between being an investor and a dealer in real estate.

irrevocable trust:
A trust that cannot be changed and, thereby, removes assets from a person's estate.

itemized deduction:
A deduction from an individual's taxable adjusted gross income that is documented on IRS Form 1040 Schedule A. An example of a specific deduction is mortgage interest.

joint tenancy:
A legal method of owning real or personal property by two or more persons in which each person owns an undivided interest in the whole and has an automatic ownership right to the property after the death of the other owner or owners. This method of ownership avoids probate but may have undesirable legal and tax consequences.

leverage:
Financial leverage is a method of increasing the return on an investment by borrowing some of the funds for the investment at an interest rate that is less than your return on the investment.

lien:
A charge or encumbrance against a property making it security for the payment of a debt, judgment, mortgage, or taxes.

like-kind exchange:
A transaction that complies with Section 1031 of the IRC that deals with tax-deferred exchanges of certain property. General rules for a tax-deferred exchange of real estate are that three possible replacement properties are identified within 45 days and one of those properties closes within 180 days, and the properties must be exchanged or qualify as a delayed tax-free exchange, qualify as like-kind property (real estate for real estate), and be held for use in a trade or business or be held as an investment.

like-kind property:
Properties that have the same nature or are similar.

limited liability company (LLC):
An entity created under state law that is taxed like a partnership but where the liability of the owners is limited to their investment in the company.

limited partner:
An investor in a partnership whose personal liability is limited and whose interest is generally considered passive for income tax purposes.

living trust:
A trust that is created and may be changed or terminated during the trust-maker's lifetime as long as he or she is competent. The trust becomes irrevocable upon the trustmaker's death. This type of trust is used primarily to avoid probate and manage property, but it does not offer any tax savings.

loan-to-value ratio (LTV):

The portion of the amount borrowed compared to the cost or value of the property purchased—that is, mortgage debt divided by the value of the property. Lenders are often constrained as to the maximum loan-to-value ratio on loans they originate. Loans on commercial property by pension funds, banks, and insurance companies are typically limited to a maximum of 70–80 percent of value. Loans on owner-occupied houses or condominiums may reach a 90–95 percent ratio when mortgage insurance is used.

material participation:

Regular, substantial, and continuous involvement in a business on the part of either the taxpayer and/or spouse that allows losses from a trade or business to be deducted without limitation under the passive loss rules.

modified adjusted gross income:

Your AGI computed without considering any passive activity loss, IRA or SEP plans, taxable social security, or the deduction for one-half of the self-employment tax.

mortgage:

A loan that is secured by real estate. The term actually refers to a security interest creating a lien, whether called a mortgage, deed of trust, security deed, or other terms used in a particular jurisdiction.

net operating income or loss:

Earnings minus operating expenses but before taxes and interest are subtracted.

ninety-five percent rule:

An IRS rule that allows any number of properties to be treated as replacement property in a like-kind exchange if the fair market value of the properties actually received by the end of the exchange period is at least 95 percent of the aggregate fair market value of all potential replacement properties identified.

nonprobate property:
Property owned by a decedent or in which the decedent had an interest on the date of her death that passes to an heir by provisions other than a will or the laws of intestacy; for example, assets held jointly or by a trust.

nonrecourse loan:
A loan where the debtor does not assume personal responsibility for the loan.

note:
See *promissory note.*

180-day period:
Refers to the 180 days the IRS gives an exchanger to complete the acquisition of a replacement property to qualify for a like-kind exchange. The first day of the 180-day period is the day after the transfer of the relinquished property.

1031 exchange:
See *like-kind exchange.*

option:
The right to buy, sell, or lease a property at a certain price for a limited period of time. If the terms of the agreement allow it, the option itself may be bought or sold.

passive activity:
For tax purposes, these activities include real estate rentals, regardless of participation, and trades or businesses where you do not materially participate. Losses are limited to passive income plus a special $25,000 allowance for rental real estate.

passive income:
Income from an activity in which you do not actively participate. The distinction between active and passive income is critical because passive losses can only be taken against passive income, not active income.

personal property:
An asset that is moveable, such as furniture and equipment.

points:
Payments to secure a loan, stated as a percentage of the borrowed amount. For example, 1 point is 1% of the loan.

power of attorney:
The written document that authorizes someone, known as an attorney-in-fact, to act for another person. The authorized actions can include signing legal documents and writing checks. If the document gives the attorney-in-fact authority to act on all matters, it is a general power of attorney. If the document limits the attorney-in-fact's authority to specific matters (for example, selling a particular piece of real estate), then it is a limited or special power of attorney.

principal:
The loan amount before interest and other fees are added to the balance.

principal residence:
The dwelling where the borrower maintains his or her permanent place of abode and typically spends the majority of the calendar year. A person may only have one principal residence at one time for tax purposes.

private annuity:
A means of transferring property to heirs that freezes the gift and estate tax value of appreciating property to the value at the date of a sale. The property owner transfers real estate to children or other family members and reserves the right to receive a fixed annuity amount each year until his death.

private letter ruling:
Written pronouncements from the IRS interpreting the Internal Revenue Code with respect to a specific set of facts and circumstances that arise from a taxpayer's request to interpret the law. Where the tax consequences are substantial and justify the legal costs, it is often advisable to obtain a private letter ruling before engaging in a transaction.

probate:
The judicial process of proving a will is valid and administering the estate of a deceased person. Avoiding probate is often desirable given the statutory and court fees, costs of hiring attorneys, executors, and administrators, and the delays that are incurred in the process.

probate property:
Assets owned by the decedent in his or her name alone or as tenant in common on the date of his or her death that pass by will or the laws of intestacy to another party.

promissory note:
A written promise by a person (known as the maker, obligor, payor, or promisor) to pay another person (known as the obligee, payee, or promisee) a sum of money (the principal) that usually includes interest to be charged on the unpaid principal amount.

qualified intermediary:
An individual or legal entity in a like-kind exchange that satisfies certain IRS rules and is permitted to hold money or title to property for a short time to facilitate an exchange transaction.

qualified personal residence trust (QPRT):
A type of irrevocable trust where a homeowner transfers ownership of the residence to a trustee but retains the right to live in the residence for a specified period of time. At the end of the specified time period, ownership of the residence transfers to the beneficiary of the trust and is valued at a substantial discount for estate tax purposes.

qualified retirement plan:
An employer-sponsored plan that meets requirements specified in the Internal Revenue Code with respect to eligibility, participation, and benefits and is qualified to receive preferential tax treatment. A qualified retirement plan may be either a defined benefit plan or a defined contribution plan such as a 401(k).

qualified terminable interest property (QTIP):
Property that qualifies for the marital deduction provided the property passes from a decedent to a surviving spouse, the surviving spouse has a qualified income interest for life in the property, and the executor of the decedent's estate makes an irrevocable election to qualify the property for the marital deduction.

real estate, or real property:
A group of rights that includes all land, structures, and items firmly attached to the land and structures, and all interests in the property, such as water rights, drilling rights, and easements.

real estate investment trust (REIT):
A privately held or publicly traded company that owns income-producing commercial real estate or real estate notes. A qualified REIT is exempt from paying corporate income taxes provided that the REIT receives a large majority of its income from real estate and annually distributes a majority of its earnings to shareholders.

real estate professional:
A person who meets the IRS requirements for spending a certain amount of time devoted to real estate and materially participates in managing investment property and is therefore able to take income tax deductions for investment property.

Realtor:
A trademark associated with someone who brokers real estate transactions and is a member of the National Association of Realtors.

realized gain:
The difference between the sales price received for a property and the adjusted basis.

recognized gain:
A portion of the realized gain that is required to be reported as income on a federal income tax return.

related parties:
The parties related to the exchanger as defined by IRC Section 267(b) and Section 707(b)(1). The definition includes, but is not limited to, a spouse, ancestors, descendants, and brothers and sisters. It does not include aunts, uncles, cousins, nieces and nephews, in-laws, ex-spouses, employees, business associates, and friends. Corporations and partnerships are related parties if the exchanger owns more than a 50 percent interest in such entities.

relinquished property:
Property an exchanger transfers in a like-kind exchange.

replacement property:
Property an exchanger identifies and ultimately receives in a like-kind exchange.

revenue ruling:
This is an official IRS interpretation of the Internal Revenue Code or regulations on a specific issue.

reverse exchange:
A type of like-kind exchange where the exchanger receives replacement property before surrendering the relinquished property.

revocable living trust:
See *living trust.*

right of survivorship:
In jointly held property, the right of one owner to automatically take title to the property on the death of the other owner.

S corporation:
A corporation that is not taxed as a separate entity. Instead, the income, losses, and credits are passed through to the shareholders.

safe harbor:
Structure approved by the IRS that if followed will produce a foreseeable tax consequence. Structuring a transaction outside the safe harbor rules creates uncertainty regarding the tax consequences of the transaction.

sales price, or net sales price:
The contract price of the property less closing costs.

self-cancelling installment note:
A means of transferring property to heirs that freezes the gift and estate tax value of appreciating property to the value at the date of a sale. The property owner transfers real estate to children or other family members on an installment basis then forgives any amounts that are unpaid on the note when he dies. The sales price is calculated using the fair market value plus a risk premium for the possibility that the seller may die before receiving all the payments.

self-directed IRA:
An IRA account in which the owner has the freedom to make decisions about particular investments.

seller financing, or seller carryback:
A financing arrangement under which the seller of property provides the buyer with the financing needed to acquire the property. The financing is often a note from the buyer secured by the property without money changing hands.

seller in a like-kind exchange:
The person who owns the replacement property before the exchange occurs.

shared equity financing agreement (SEFA):
A contract under which two or more people acquire undivided interests for more than fifty years in an entire dwelling unit, including the land. Under the agreement, one or more of the co-owners is entitled to occupy the property as his main home upon payment of rent to the other co-owner or owners.

standard deduction:
A set amount of deduction that is used to reduce a taxpayer's adjusted gross income if she does not choose the itemized deduction method of calculating taxable income.

Starker exchange:
A like-kind exchange where there is a delay between the closing of the sale of the relinquished property and the closing of the purchase of the replacement property.

stepped-up basis:
An asset's original purchase price adjusted upward for appreciation or downward for depreciation for tax purposes at the time of inheritance.

straight-line depreciation:
Depreciation where the amount for each period is equal.

taxable income:
The amount of net income (gross income minus all adjustments, deductions, and exemptions) that is used to calculate income tax owed.

tax deferred:
A term that indicates no tax is currently due on the transaction or income received. Instead, tax is due at a later date when the transaction is closed.

tax-deferred exchange:
See *like-kind exchange.*

tenancy in common:
A legal method of owning real or personal property by two or more persons in which each person's interest passes to his or her heirs or estate upon death instead of to the other co-owners. In contrast, see joint tenancy.

title:
A legal document that proves ownership of a property.

trust:
A relationship whereby one party (the trustmaker, trustor, grantor, or settlor) transfers legal title to property to another party (the trustee) to be held for the benefit of someone else (the beneficiary). There are many kinds of trusts with different terms and requirements, and the document establishing the trust is a form of trust agreement.

unrelated business income (UBI):
Earnings from trade or business activities that are regularly carried on and not substantially related to the tax-exempt purpose of a tax-exempt organization. These activities may be taxed since they are outside the scope of the tax-exempt part of the business.

Index

About the Authors

TYLER D. KRAEMER, ESQ.

Tyler is an attorney with over a decade of experience in real estate, business, intellectual property, and estate planning law. His clients include real estate investors, developers, and brokers as well as financial institutions, Internet-based companies, and international consulting firms. He is also outside legal counsel to a large Realtor® association and a multiple listing service (MLS). Tyler is regularly interviewed by publications across the United States on real estate–related issues. In addition, Tyler has significant personal experience with investing in and developing real estate. He is also coauthor of *The Complete Guide to Reverse Mortgages* (2007 Adams Media). Tyler lives in Colorado with his wife, Tammy, and their two children.

TAMMY H. KRAEMER, ESQ.

Tammy is an attorney with over a decade of experience in business, real estate, and intellectual property law. She served as general counsel for an established software company with worldwide offices. Prior to that time, Tammy worked at a large regional law firm in their corporate law and securities department. In addition to real estate–related legal work, Tammy has personal experience with investing in and developing real estate. She has written numerous articles and is coauthor of another book titled *The Complete Guide to Reverse Mortgages* (2007 Adams Media). Tammy lives in Colorado with her husband, Tyler, and their two children.